W

WORLD WAR X

1 / HELIUS

WRITTEN BY

Jerry Frissen

ART BY

Peter Snejbjerg

COLORS BY

Delphine Rieu

Titan
COMICS

WORLD WAR X

WRITTEN BY
Jerry Frissen

ART BY
Peter Snejbjerg

COLORS BY
Delphine Rieu

TRANSLATED BY
Edward Gauvin

LETTERING BY
Kirsten Murray

For Laila.

PETER

TITAN COMICS

COLLECTION EDITOR
Nora Goldberg
COLLECTION DESIGNER
Russell Seal
SENIOR EDITOR
Steve White
TITAN COMICS EDITORIAL
Andrew James, Tom Williams
PRODUCTION MANAGER
Obi Onuora
PRODUCTION SUPERVISORS
Jackie Flook, Maria Pearson
PRODUCTION ASSISTANT
Peter James
STUDIO MANAGER
Emma Smith
CIRCULATION MANAGER
Steve Tothill
MARKETING MANAGER
Ricky Claydon
SENIOR MARKETING AND PRESS EXECUTIVE
Owen Johnson
PUBLISHING MANAGER
Darryl Tothill
PUBLISHING DIRECTOR
Chris Teather
OPERATIONS DIRECTOR
Leigh Baulch
EXECUTIVE DIRECTOR
Vivian Cheung
PUBLISHER
Nick Landau

World War X Volume 1: Helius
ISBN: 9781782761129

Published by Titan Comics
A division of Titan Publishing Group Ltd.
144 Southwark St.
London
SE1 0UP

A CIP catalogue record for this title is available from the British Library.

First edition: April 2015

Originally published in 2013 by Le Lombard, France as *World War X 1 - Hélius.*

10 9 8 7 6 5 4 3 2 1

Printed in China.
Titan Comics. TC0210

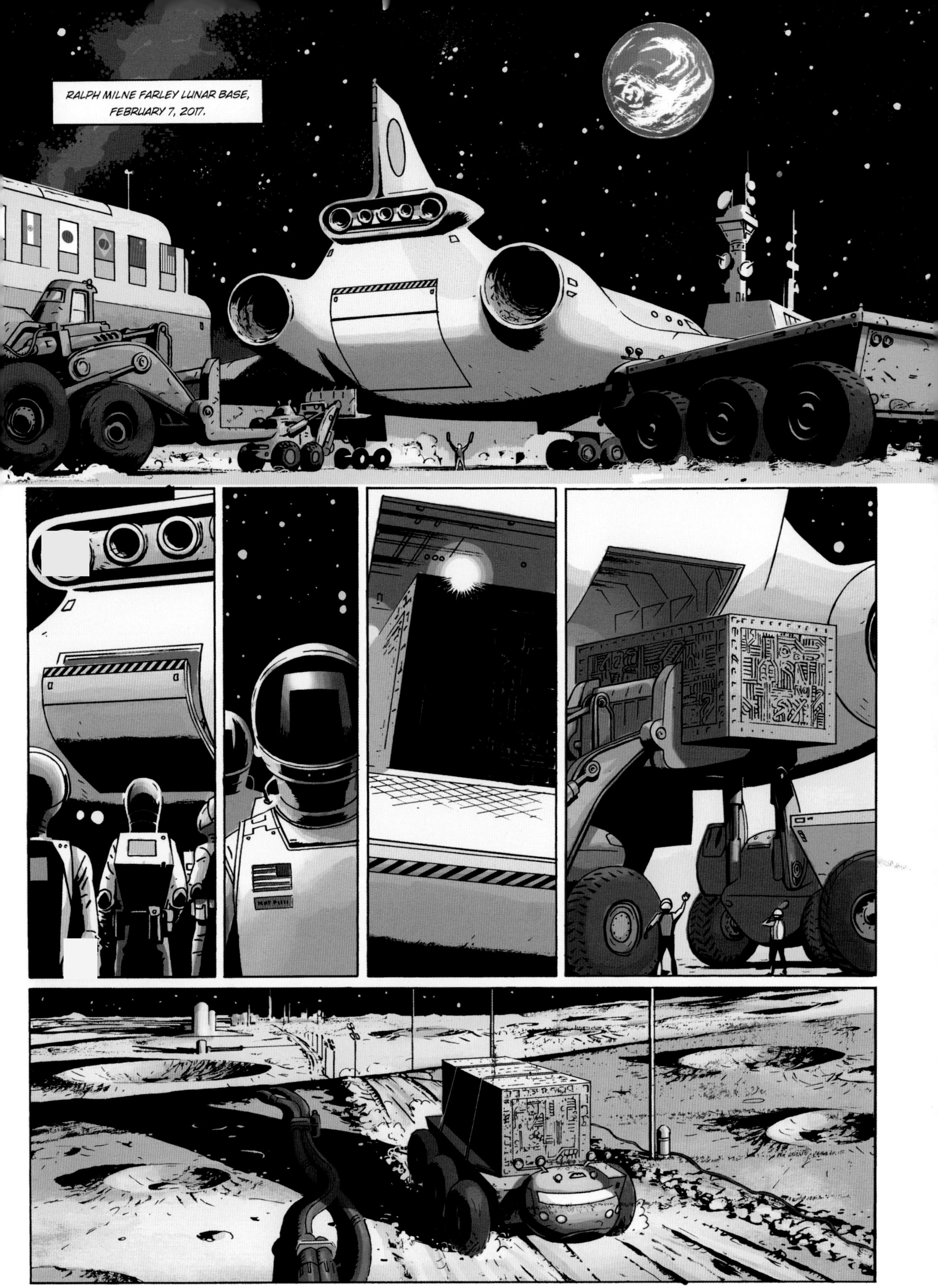
RALPH MILNE FARLEY LUNAR BASE,
FEBRUARY 7, 2017.

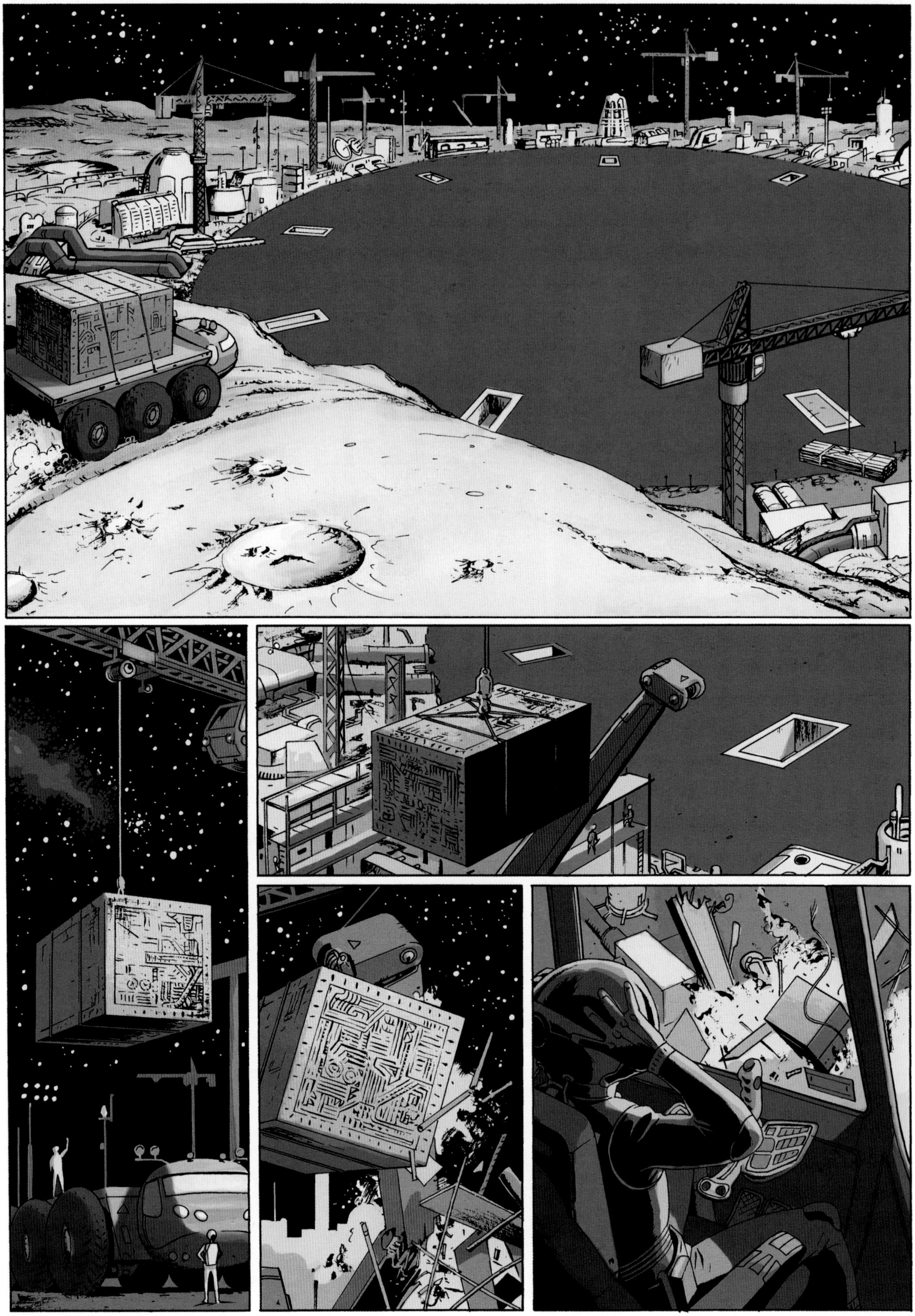

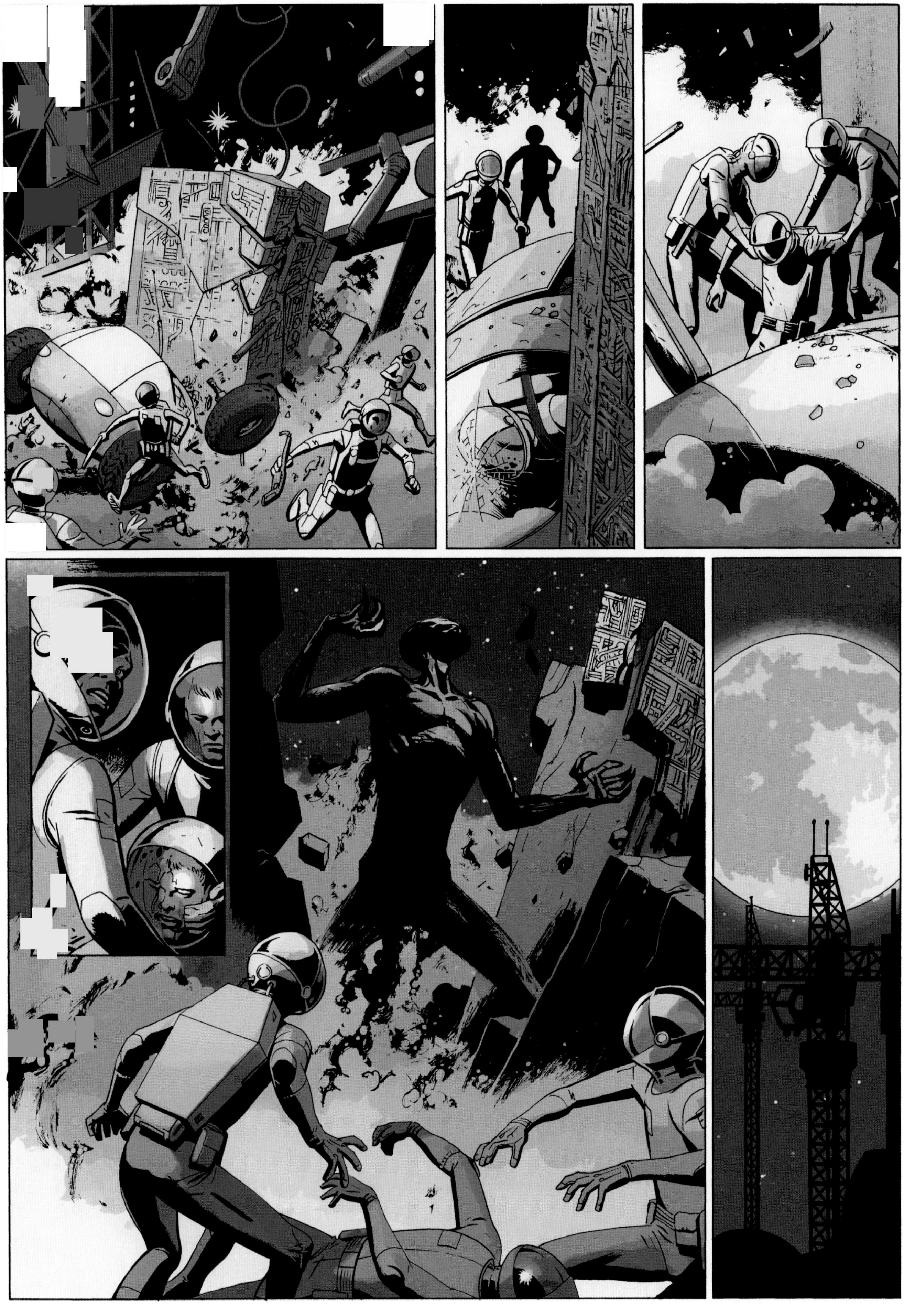

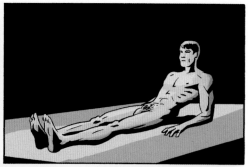

DOUGLAS COUNTY, OREGON, USA. FEBRUARY 7, 2017.

WORLD WAR X
HELIUS

JUNGLE, PAPUA NEW GUINEA, FEBRUARY 7, 2017.

BUT HOW IS THAT POSSIBLE? IT'S COMPLETELY ABSURD.

THERE ARE ALMOST A THOUSAND PEOPLE ON THE MOON! WE CAN'T JUST HAVE LOST CONTACT...

FINE, KEEP ME INFORMED.

HOW FAR TO THE BASE?

NO MORE THAN AN HOUR.

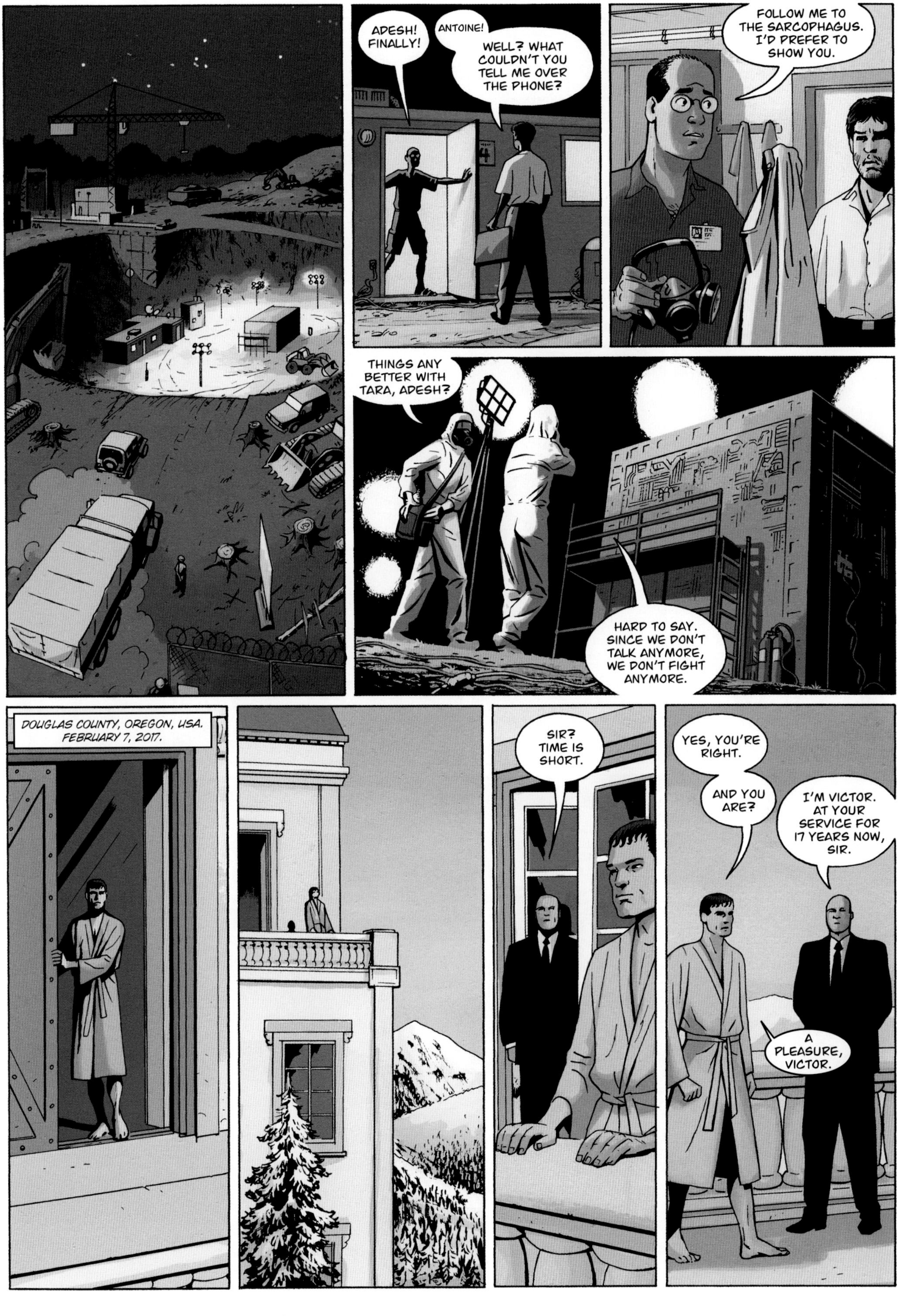

ADESH! FINALLY!
ANTOINE!
WELL? WHAT COULDN'T YOU TELL ME OVER THE PHONE?
FOLLOW ME TO THE SARCOPHAGUS. I'D PREFER TO SHOW YOU.
THINGS ANY BETTER WITH TARA, ADESH?
HARD TO SAY. SINCE WE DON'T TALK ANYMORE, WE DON'T FIGHT ANYMORE.
DOUGLAS COUNTY, OREGON, USA. FEBRUARY 7, 2017.
SIR? TIME IS SHORT.
YES, YOU'RE RIGHT.
AND YOU ARE?
I'M VICTOR. AT YOUR SERVICE FOR 17 YEARS NOW, SIR.
A PLEASURE, VICTOR.

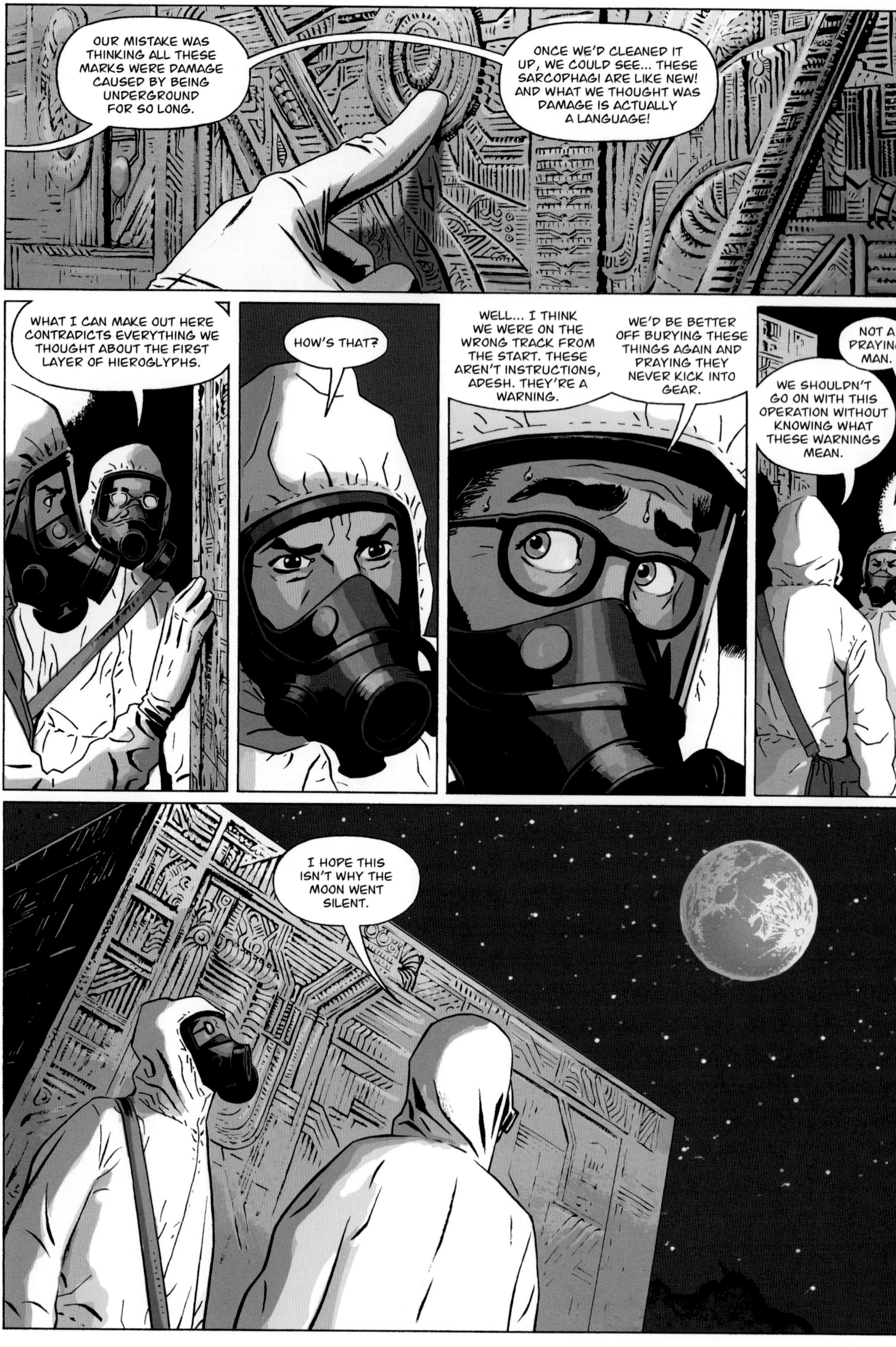
OUR MISTAKE WAS THINKING ALL THESE MARKS WERE DAMAGE CAUSED BY BEING UNDERGROUND FOR SO LONG.
ONCE WE'D CLEANED IT UP, WE COULD SEE... THESE SARCOPHAGI ARE LIKE NEW! AND WHAT WE THOUGHT WAS DAMAGE IS ACTUALLY A LANGUAGE!
WHAT I CAN MAKE OUT HERE CONTRADICTS EVERYTHING WE THOUGHT ABOUT THE FIRST LAYER OF HIEROGLYPHS.
HOW'S THAT?
WELL... I THINK WE WERE ON THE WRONG TRACK FROM THE START. THESE AREN'T INSTRUCTIONS, ADESH. THEY'RE A WARNING.
WE'D BE BETTER OFF BURYING THESE THINGS AGAIN AND PRAYING THEY NEVER KICK INTO GEAR.
NOT A PRAYING MAN.
WE SHOULDN'T GO ON WITH THIS OPERATION WITHOUT KNOWING WHAT THESE WARNINGS MEAN.
I HOPE THIS ISN'T WHY THE MOON WENT SILENT.

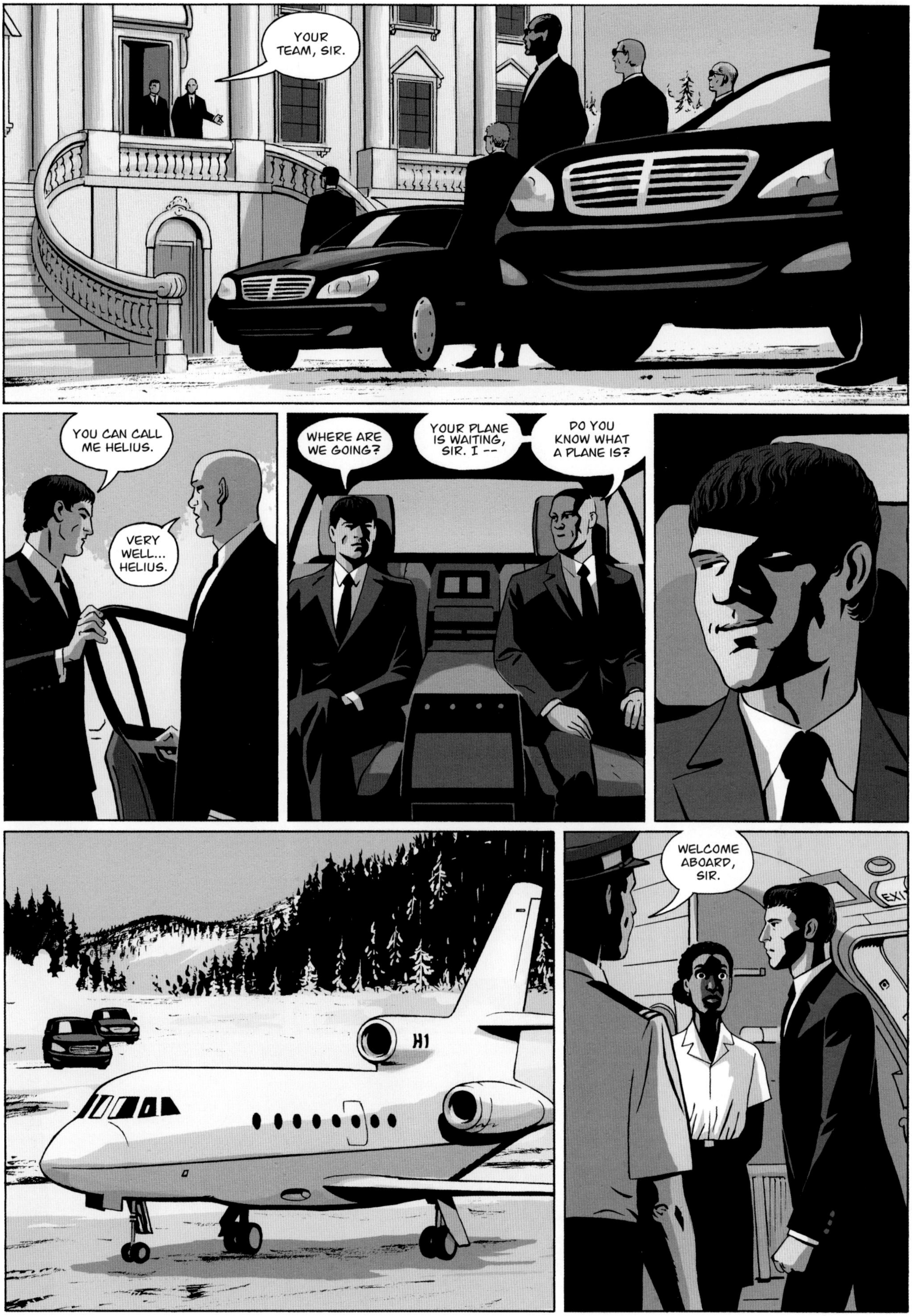
YOUR TEAM, SIR.
YOU CAN CALL ME HELIUS.
VERY WELL... HELIUS.
WHERE ARE WE GOING?
YOUR PLANE IS WAITING, SIR. I --
DO YOU KNOW WHAT A PLANE IS?
H1
WELCOME ABOARD, SIR.
EXIT

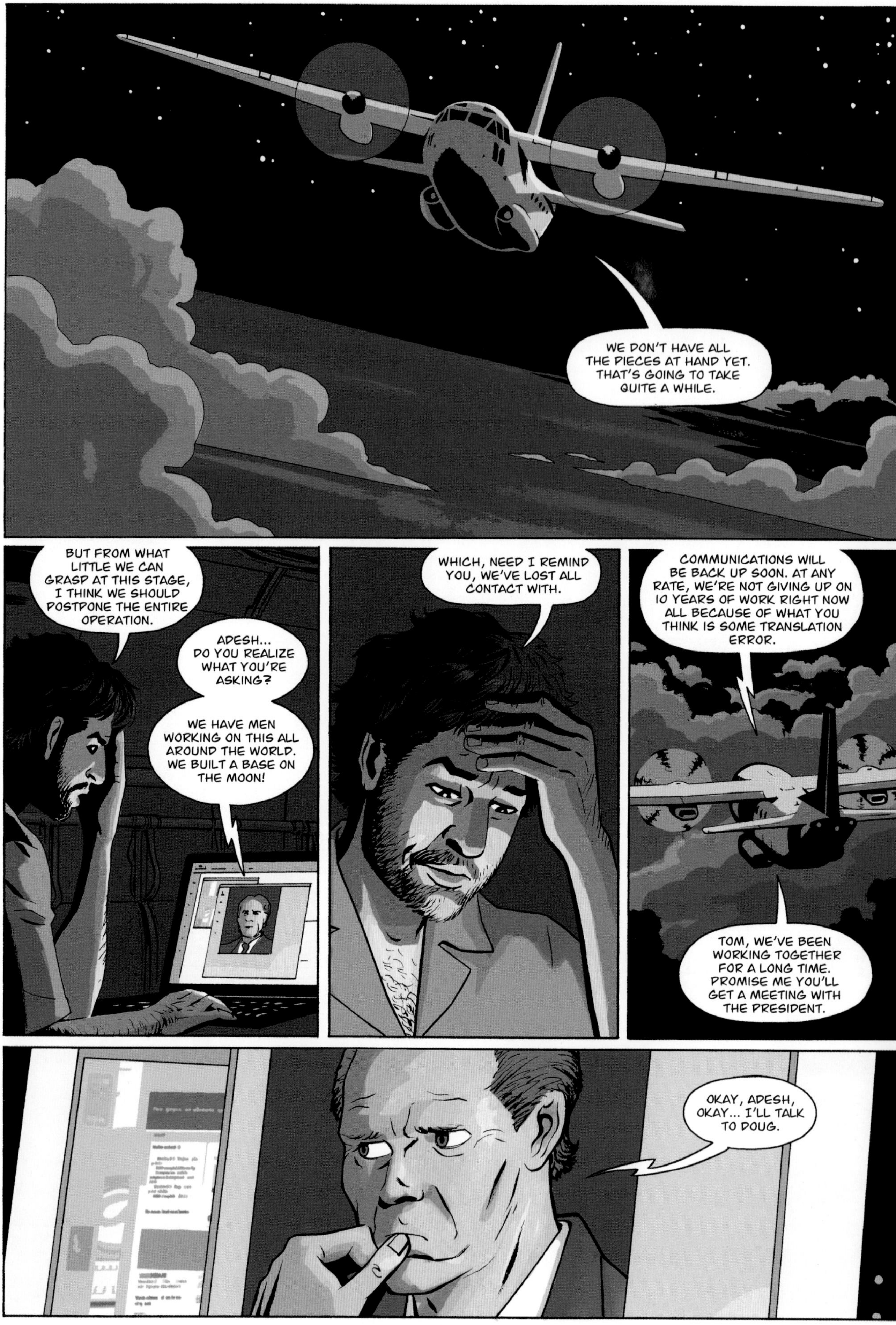
WE DON'T HAVE ALL THE PIECES AT HAND YET. THAT'S GOING TO TAKE QUITE A WHILE.
BUT FROM WHAT LITTLE WE CAN GRASP AT THIS STAGE, I THINK WE SHOULD POSTPONE THE ENTIRE OPERATION.
ADESH... DO YOU REALIZE WHAT YOU'RE ASKING?
WE HAVE MEN WORKING ON THIS ALL AROUND THE WORLD. WE BUILT A BASE ON THE MOON!
WHICH, NEED I REMIND YOU, WE'VE LOST ALL CONTACT WITH.
COMMUNICATIONS WILL BE BACK UP SOON. AT ANY RATE, WE'RE NOT GIVING UP ON 10 YEARS OF WORK RIGHT NOW ALL BECAUSE OF WHAT YOU THINK IS SOME TRANSLATION ERROR.
TOM, WE'VE BEEN WORKING TOGETHER FOR A LONG TIME. PROMISE ME YOU'LL GET A MEETING WITH THE PRESIDENT.
OKAY, ADESH, OKAY... I'LL TALK TO DOUG.

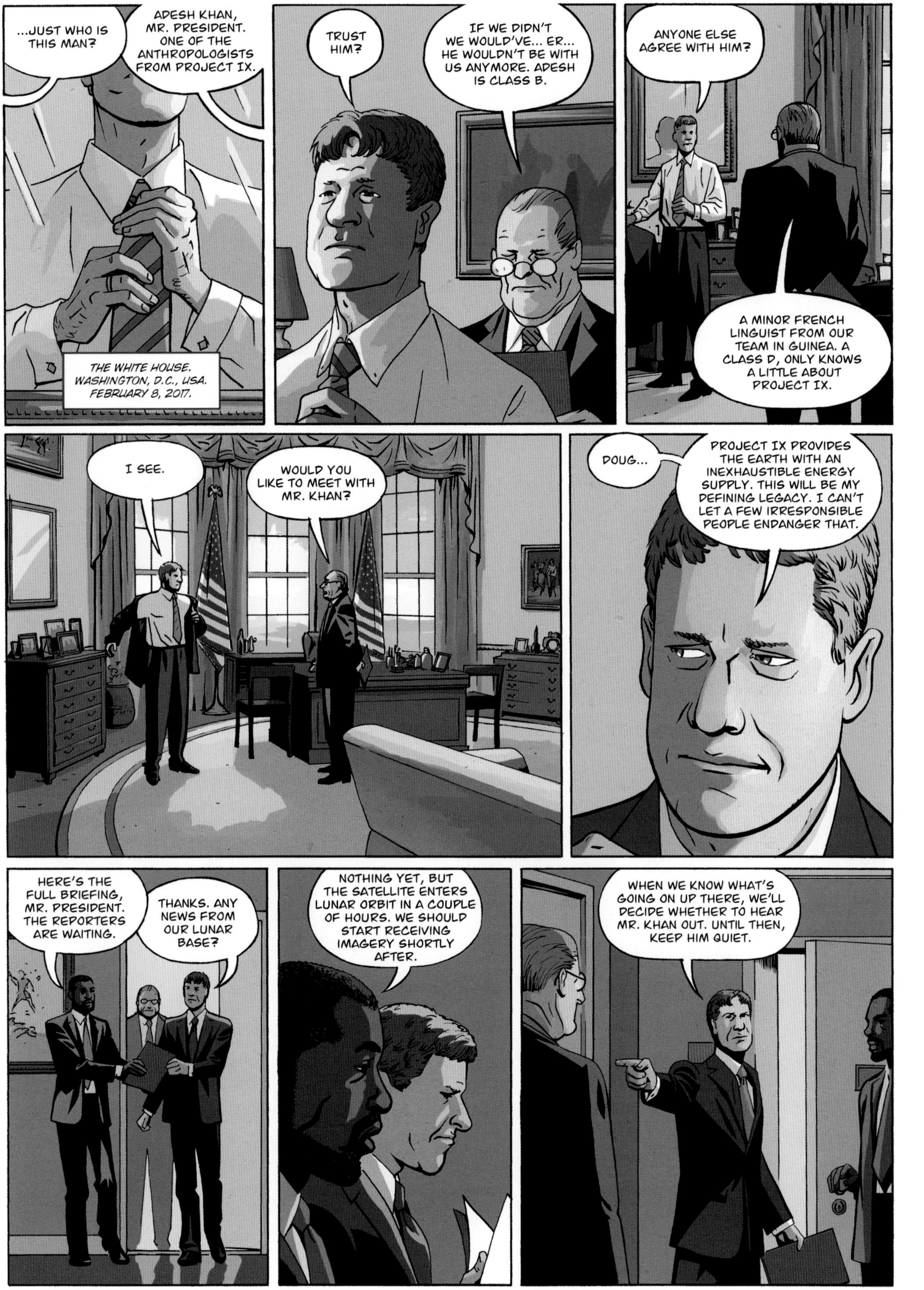
...JUST WHO IS THIS MAN?
ADESH KHAN, MR. PRESIDENT. ONE OF THE ANTHROPOLOGISTS FROM PROJECT IX.
THE WHITE HOUSE. WASHINGTON, D.C., USA. FEBRUARY 8, 2017.
TRUST HIM?
IF WE DIDN'T WE WOULD'VE... ER... HE WOULDN'T BE WITH US ANYMORE. ADESH IS CLASS B.
ANYONE ELSE AGREE WITH HIM?
A MINOR FRENCH LINGUIST FROM OUR TEAM IN GUINEA. A CLASS D, ONLY KNOWS A LITTLE ABOUT PROJECT IX.
I SEE.
WOULD YOU LIKE TO MEET WITH MR. KHAN?
DOUG...
PROJECT IX PROVIDES THE EARTH WITH AN INEXHAUSTIBLE ENERGY SUPPLY. THIS WILL BE MY DEFINING LEGACY. I CAN'T LET A FEW IRRESPONSIBLE PEOPLE ENDANGER THAT.
HERE'S THE FULL BRIEFING, MR. PRESIDENT. THE REPORTERS ARE WAITING.
THANKS. ANY NEWS FROM OUR LUNAR BASE?
NOTHING YET, BUT THE SATELLITE ENTERS LUNAR ORBIT IN A COUPLE OF HOURS. WE SHOULD START RECEIVING IMAGERY SHORTLY AFTER.
WHEN WE KNOW WHAT'S GOING ON UP THERE, WE'LL DECIDE WHETHER TO HEAR MR. KHAN OUT. UNTIL THEN, KEEP HIM QUIET.

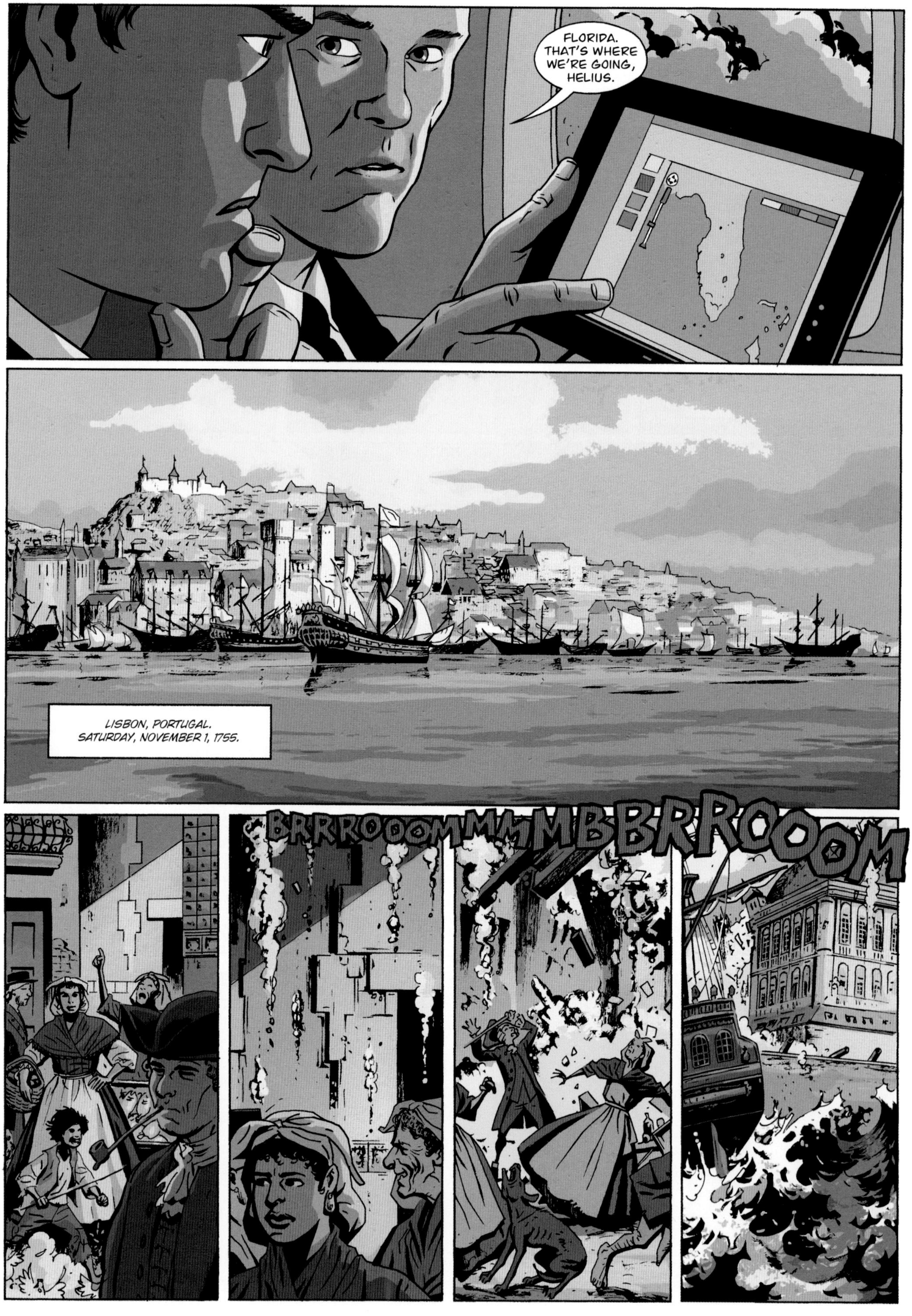
FLORIDA. THAT'S WHERE WE'RE GOING, HELIUS.
LISBON, PORTUGAL.
SATURDAY, NOVEMBER 1, 1755.
BRRROOOMMMMMBBRROOOM

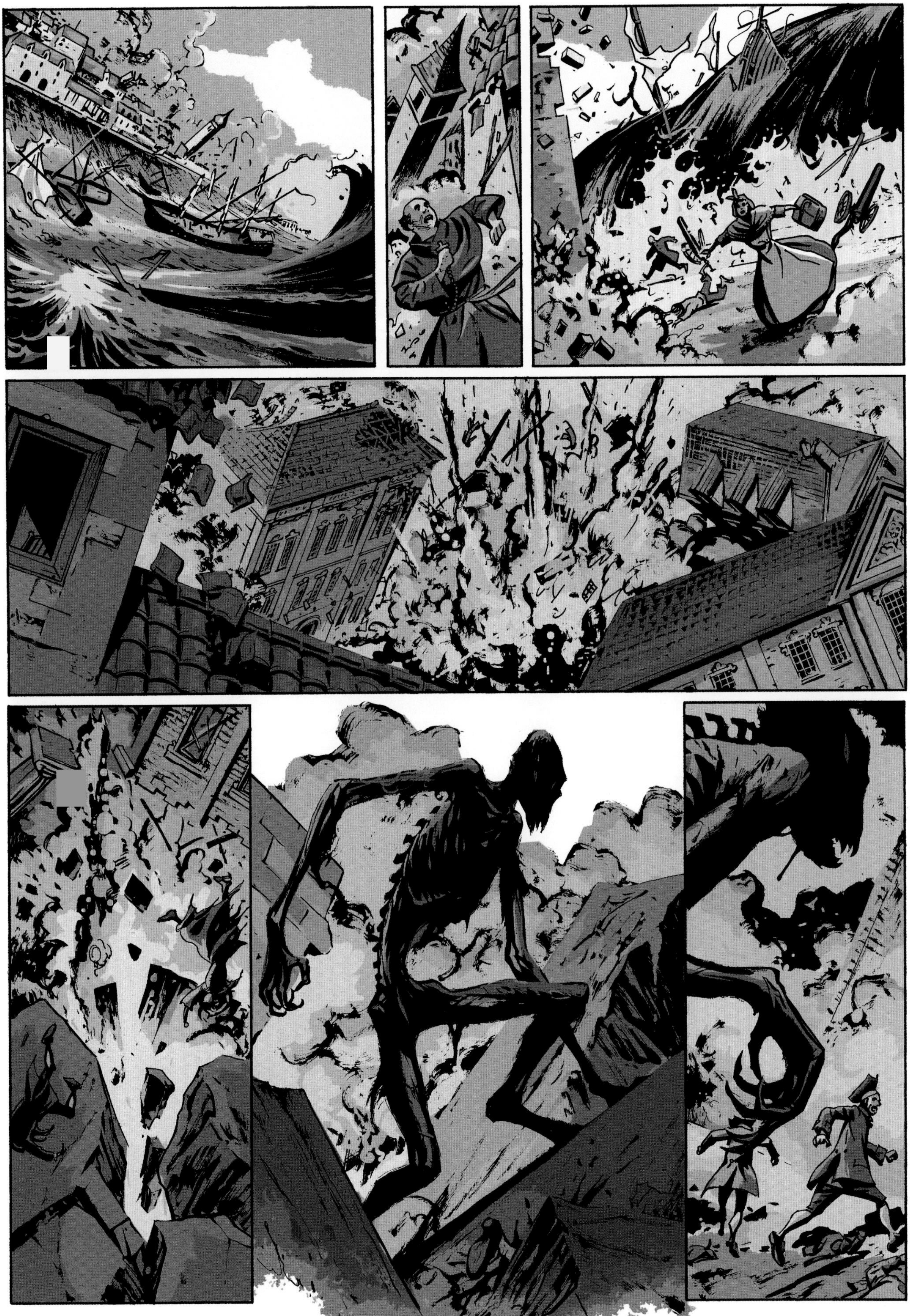

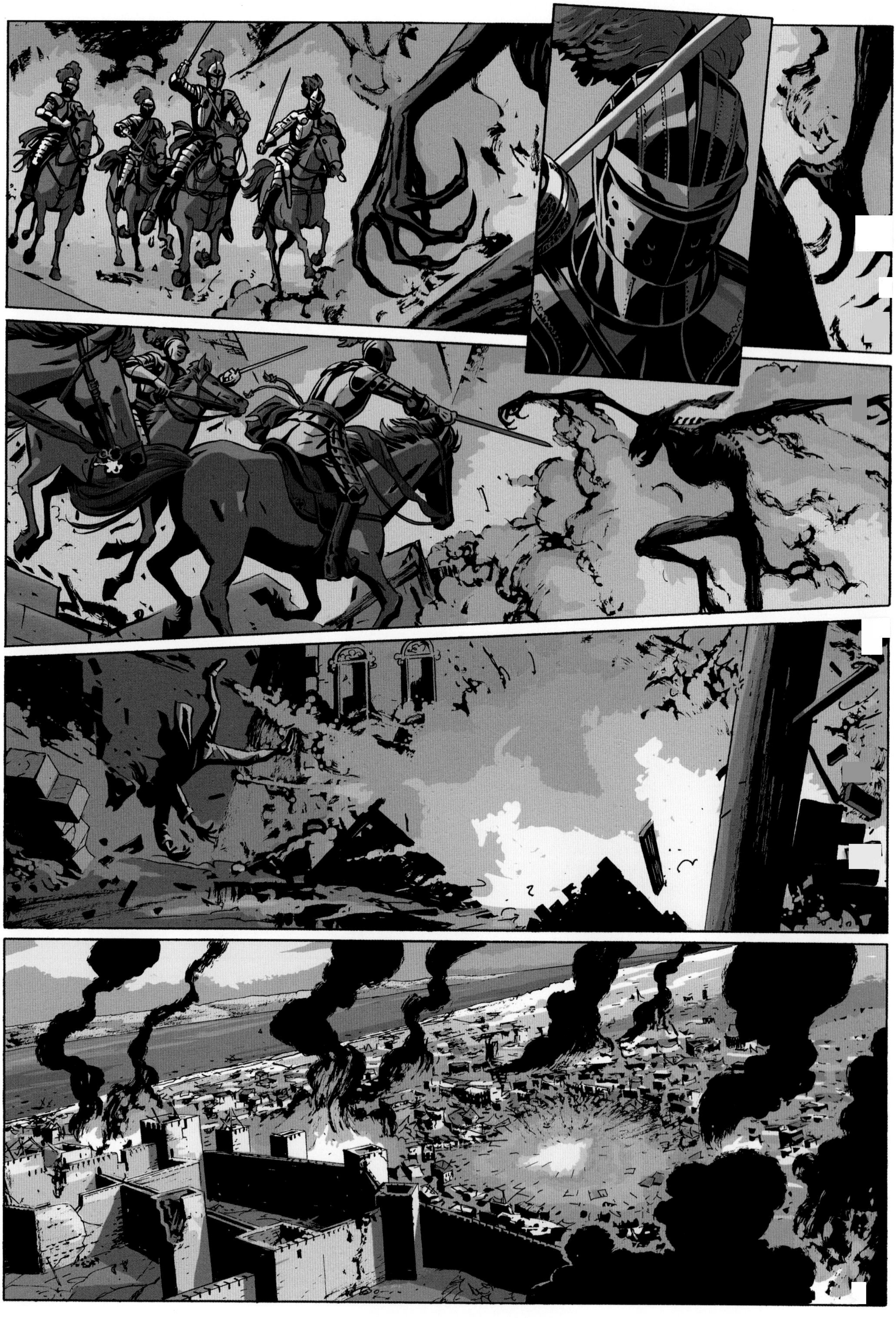

MORE LIGHT OVER HERE.

RALPH MILNE FARLEY LUNAR BASE, FEBRUARY 8, 2017.

I SAID I NEEDED MORE LIGHT. WHAT THE HELL ARE YOU--

FRED, LOOK! OUTSIDE!

WHAT THE-- ?

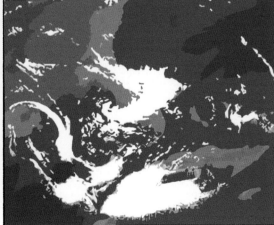

15

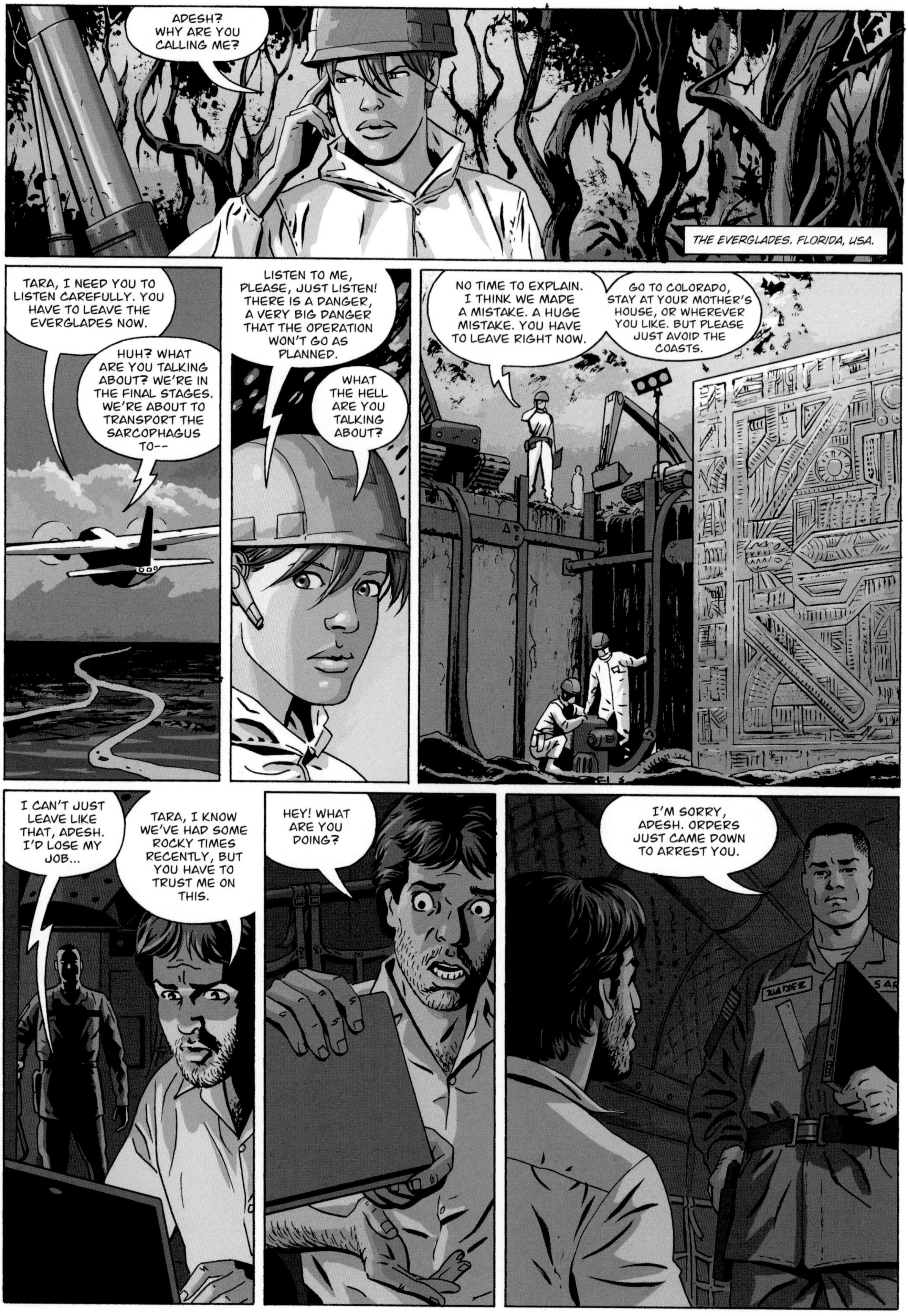
ADESH? WHY ARE YOU CALLING ME?
THE EVERGLADES, FLORIDA, USA.
TARA, I NEED YOU TO LISTEN CAREFULLY. YOU HAVE TO LEAVE THE EVERGLADES NOW.
HUH? WHAT ARE YOU TALKING ABOUT? WE'RE IN THE FINAL STAGES. WE'RE ABOUT TO TRANSPORT THE SARCOPHAGUS TO--
LISTEN TO ME, PLEASE, JUST LISTEN! THERE IS A DANGER, A VERY BIG DANGER THAT THE OPERATION WON'T GO AS PLANNED.
WHAT THE HELL ARE YOU TALKING ABOUT?
NO TIME TO EXPLAIN. I THINK WE MADE A MISTAKE. A HUGE MISTAKE. YOU HAVE TO LEAVE RIGHT NOW.
GO TO COLORADO, STAY AT YOUR MOTHER'S HOUSE, OR WHEREVER YOU LIKE. BUT PLEASE JUST AVOID THE COASTS.
I CAN'T JUST LEAVE LIKE THAT, ADESH. I'D LOSE MY JOB...
TARA, I KNOW WE'VE HAD SOME ROCKY TIMES RECENTLY, BUT YOU HAVE TO TRUST ME ON THIS.
HEY! WHAT ARE YOU DOING?
I'M SORRY, ADESH. ORDERS JUST CAME DOWN TO ARREST YOU.

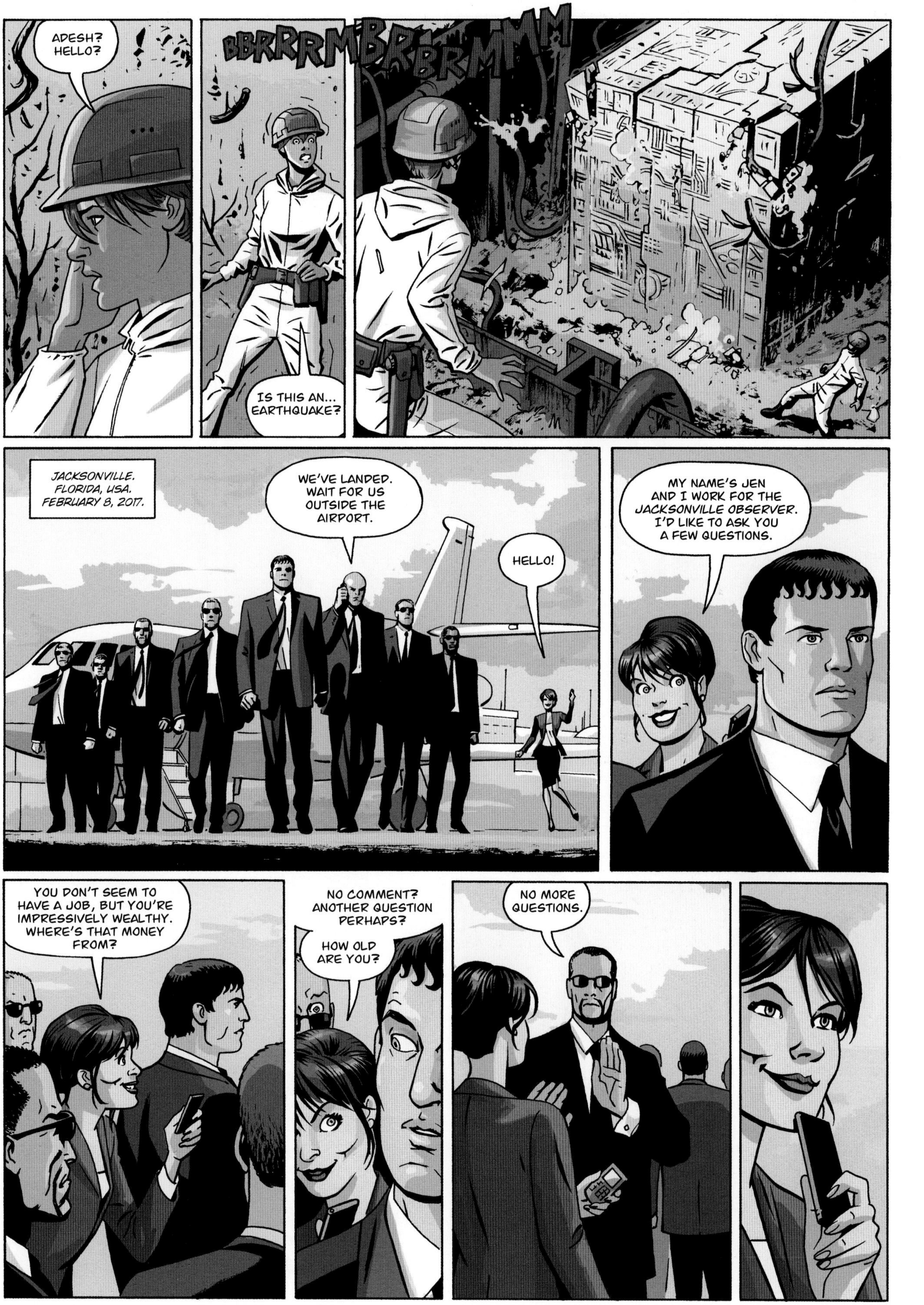
ADESH? HELLO?
BBRRRMBRRBRMMM
IS THIS AN... EARTHQUAKE?
JACKSONVILLE. FLORIDA, USA. FEBRUARY 8, 2017.
WE'VE LANDED. WAIT FOR US OUTSIDE THE AIRPORT.
HELLO!
MY NAME'S JEN AND I WORK FOR THE JACKSONVILLE OBSERVER. I'D LIKE TO ASK YOU A FEW QUESTIONS.
YOU DON'T SEEM TO HAVE A JOB, BUT YOU'RE IMPRESSIVELY WEALTHY. WHERE'S THAT MONEY FROM?
NO COMMENT? ANOTHER QUESTION PERHAPS?
HOW OLD ARE YOU?
NO MORE QUESTIONS.

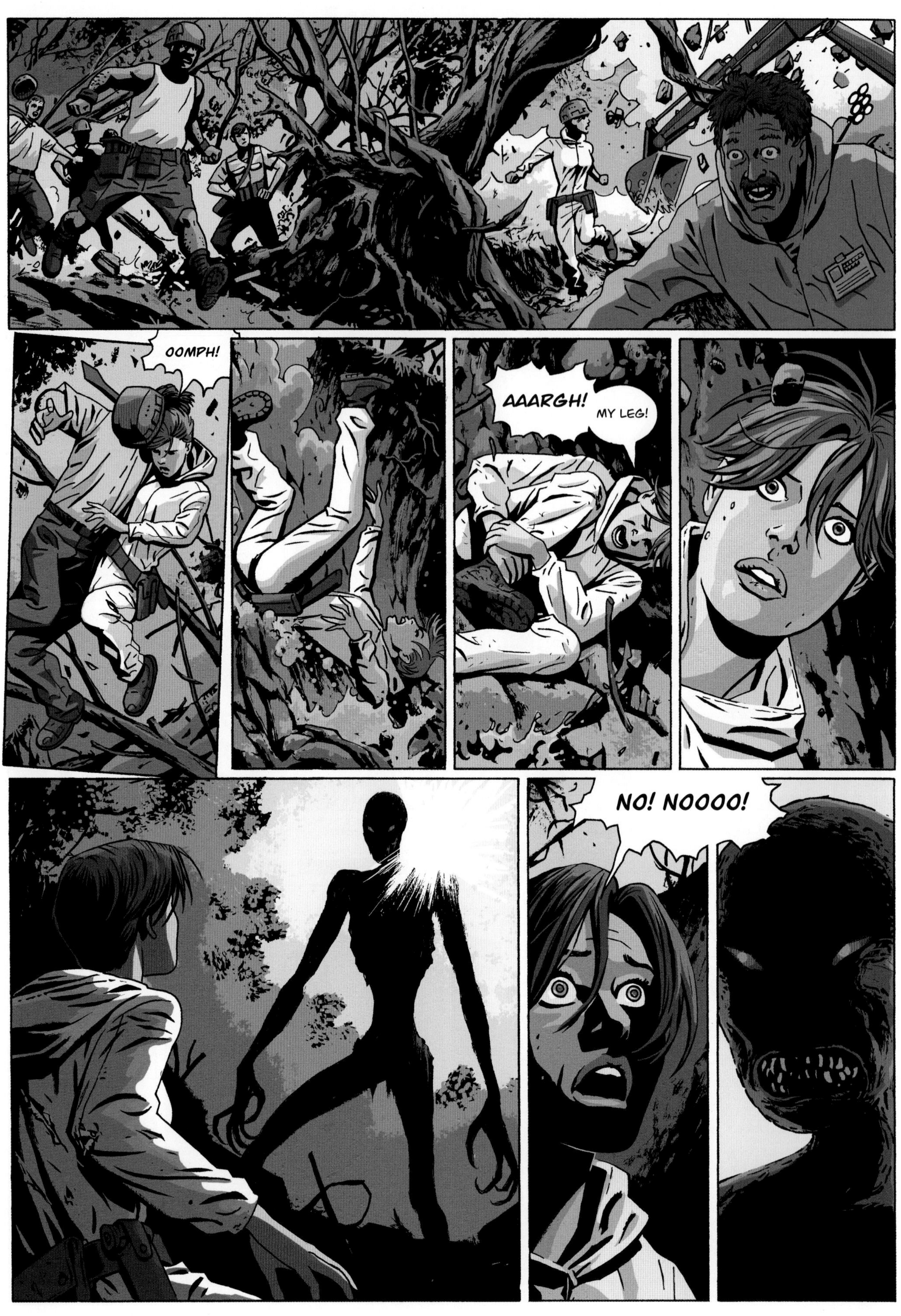
OOMPH!
AAARGH!
MY LEG!
NO! NOOOO!

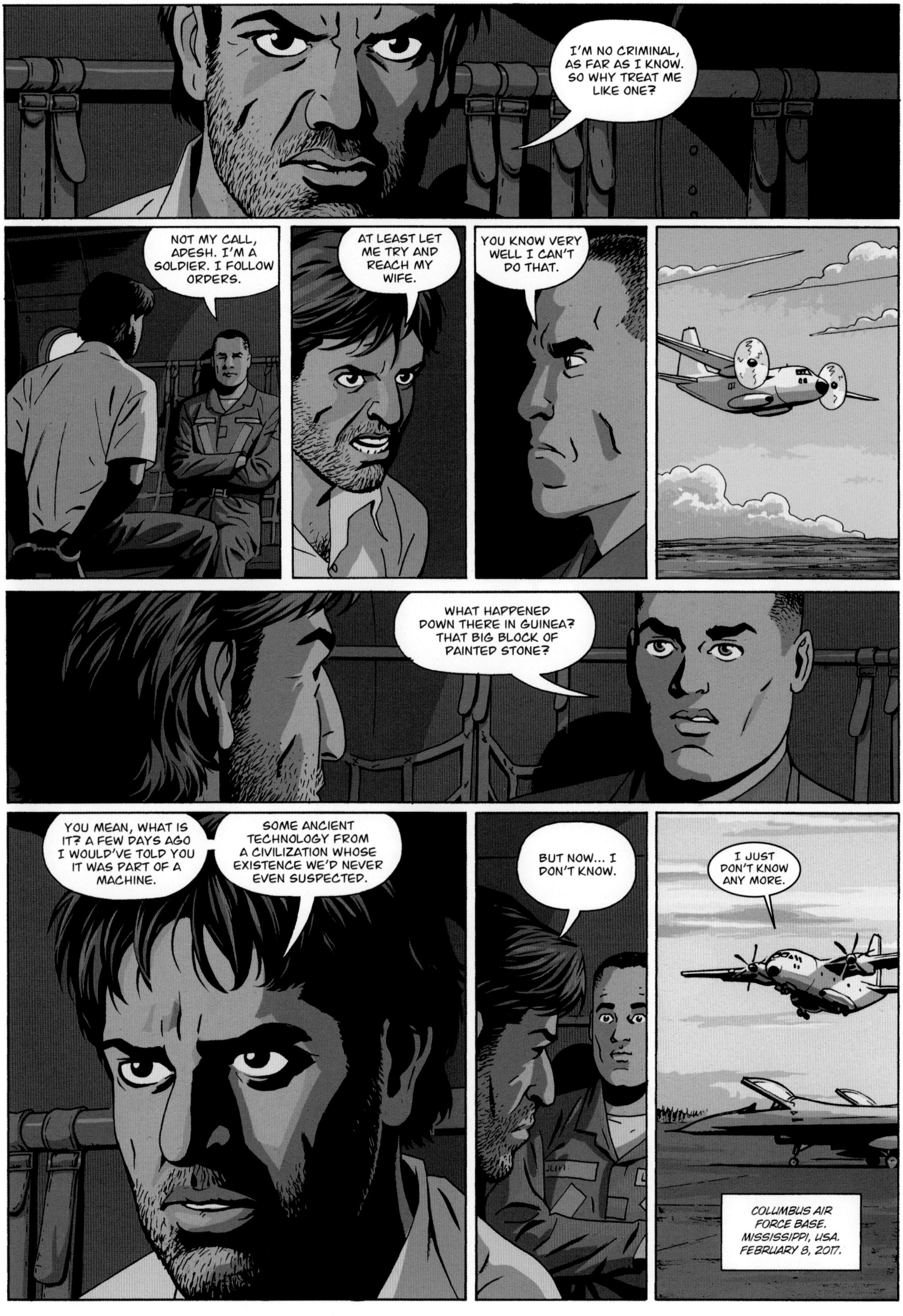
I'M NO CRIMINAL, AS FAR AS I KNOW. SO WHY TREAT ME LIKE ONE?
NOT MY CALL, ADESH. I'M A SOLDIER. I FOLLOW ORDERS.
AT LEAST LET ME TRY AND REACH MY WIFE.
YOU KNOW VERY WELL I CAN'T DO THAT.
WHAT HAPPENED DOWN THERE IN GUINEA? THAT BIG BLOCK OF PAINTED STONE?
YOU MEAN, WHAT IS IT? A FEW DAYS AGO I WOULD'VE TOLD YOU IT WAS PART OF A MACHINE.
SOME ANCIENT TECHNOLOGY FROM A CIVILIZATION WHOSE EXISTENCE WE'D NEVER EVEN SUSPECTED.
BUT NOW... I DON'T KNOW.
I JUST DON'T KNOW ANY MORE.
COLUMBUS AIR FORCE BASE. MISSISSIPPI, USA. FEBRUARY 8, 2017.

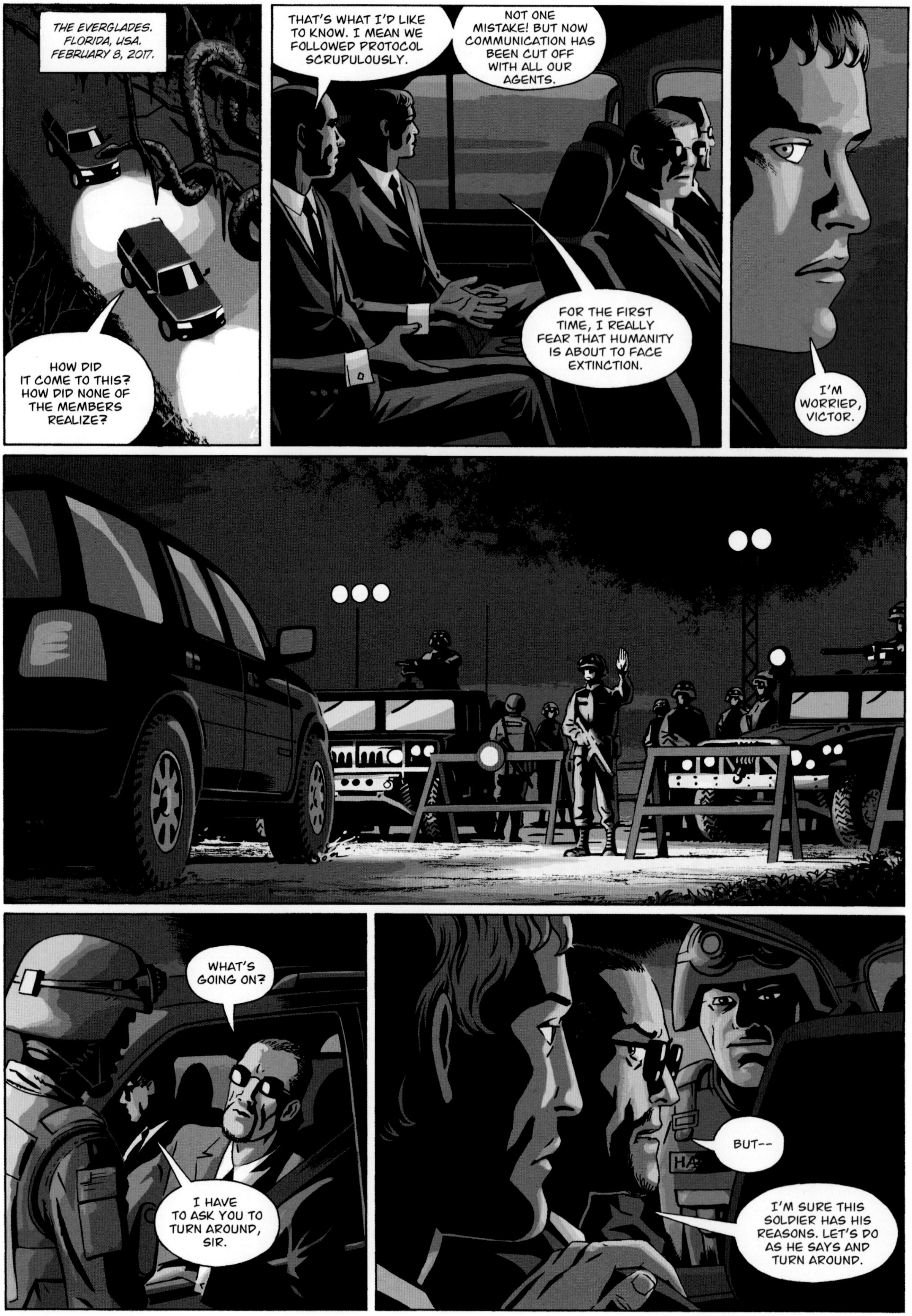
THE EVERGLADES. FLORIDA, USA. FEBRUARY 8, 2017.
HOW DID IT COME TO THIS? HOW DID NONE OF THE MEMBERS REALIZE?
THAT'S WHAT I'D LIKE TO KNOW. I MEAN WE FOLLOWED PROTOCOL SCRUPULOUSLY.
NOT ONE MISTAKE! BUT NOW COMMUNICATION HAS BEEN CUT OFF WITH ALL OUR AGENTS.
FOR THE FIRST TIME, I REALLY FEAR THAT HUMANITY IS ABOUT TO FACE EXTINCTION.
I'M WORRIED, VICTOR.
WHAT'S GOING ON?
I HAVE TO ASK YOU TO TURN AROUND, SIR.
BUT--
I'M SURE THIS SOLDIER HAS HIS REASONS. LET'S DO AS HE SAYS AND TURN AROUND.

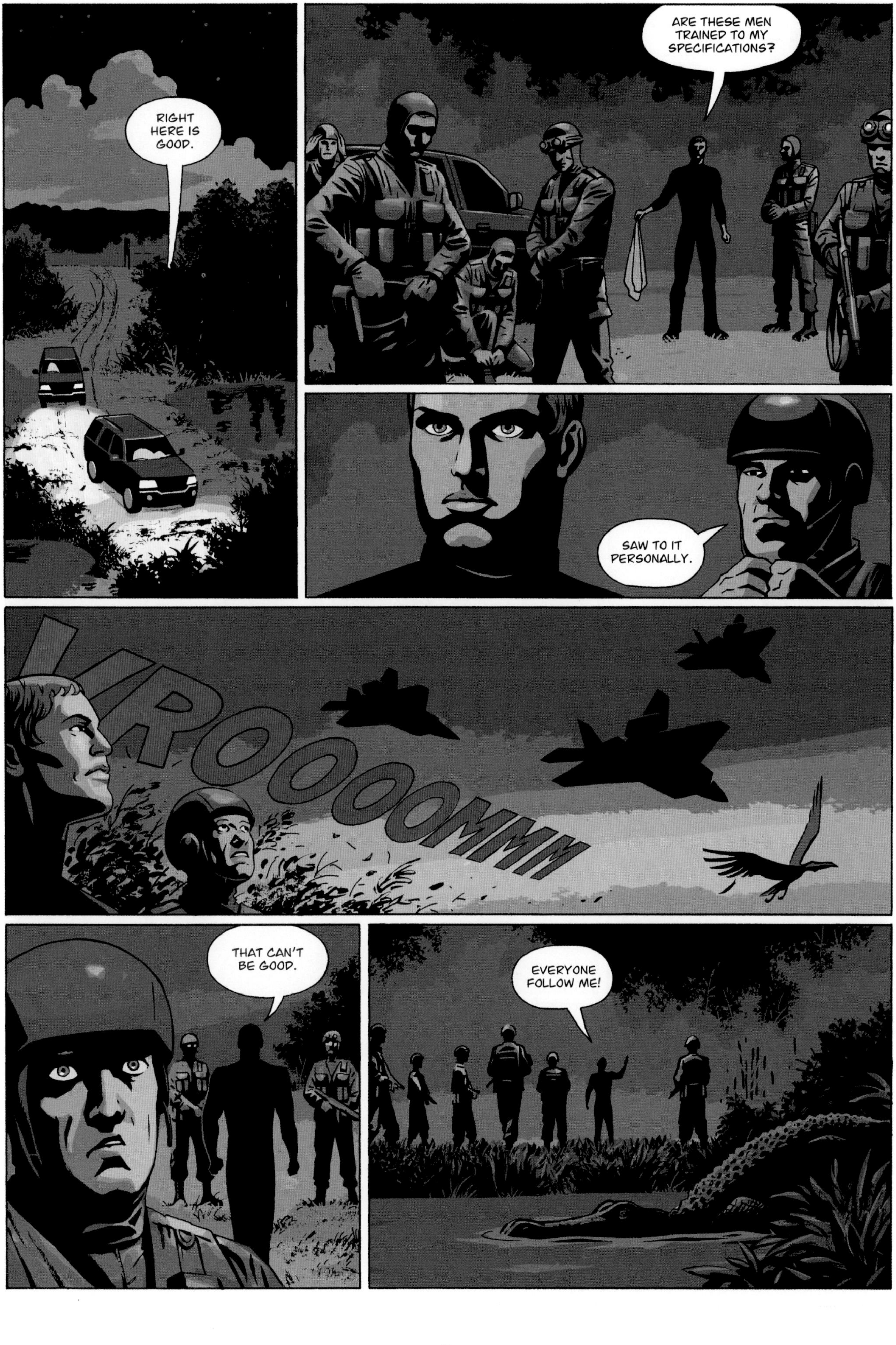
RIGHT HERE IS GOOD.
ARE THESE MEN TRAINED TO MY SPECIFICATIONS?
SAW TO IT PERSONALLY.
VROOOOMMM
THAT CAN'T BE GOOD.
EVERYONE FOLLOW ME!

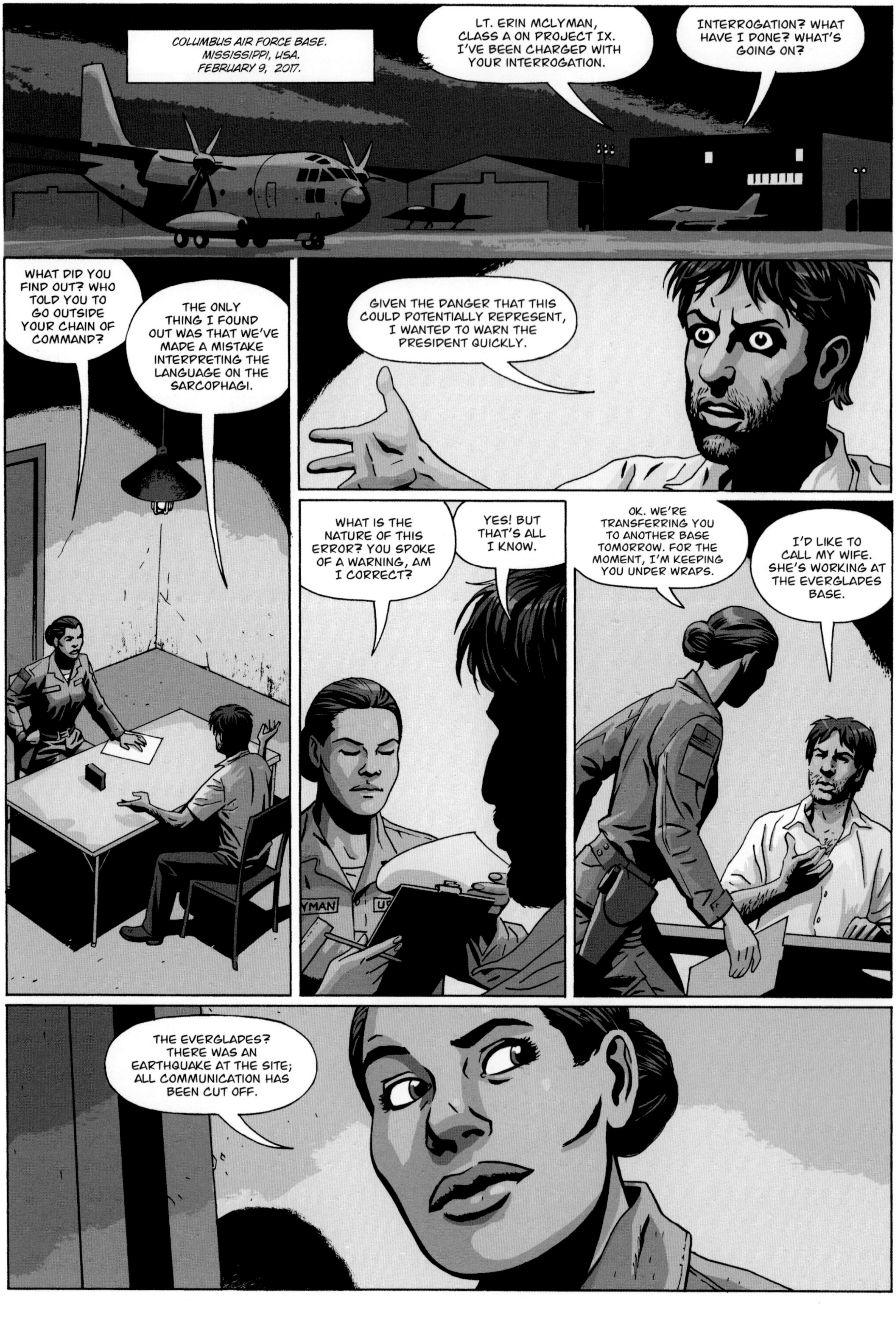
COLUMBUS AIR FORCE BASE. MISSISSIPPI, USA. FEBRUARY 9, 2017.
LT. ERIN MCLYMAN, CLASS A ON PROJECT IX. I'VE BEEN CHARGED WITH YOUR INTERROGATION.
INTERROGATION? WHAT HAVE I DONE? WHAT'S GOING ON?
WHAT DID YOU FIND OUT? WHO TOLD YOU TO GO OUTSIDE YOUR CHAIN OF COMMAND?
THE ONLY THING I FOUND OUT WAS THAT WE'VE MADE A MISTAKE INTERPRETING THE LANGUAGE ON THE SARCOPHAGI.
GIVEN THE DANGER THAT THIS COULD POTENTIALLY REPRESENT, I WANTED TO WARN THE PRESIDENT QUICKLY.
WHAT IS THE NATURE OF THIS ERROR? YOU SPOKE OF A WARNING, AM I CORRECT?
YES! BUT THAT'S ALL I KNOW.
OK. WE'RE TRANSFERRING YOU TO ANOTHER BASE TOMORROW. FOR THE MOMENT, I'M KEEPING YOU UNDER WRAPS.
I'D LIKE TO CALL MY WIFE. SHE'S WORKING AT THE EVERGLADES BASE.
THE EVERGLADES? THERE WAS AN EARTHQUAKE AT THE SITE; ALL COMMUNICATION HAS BEEN CUT OFF.

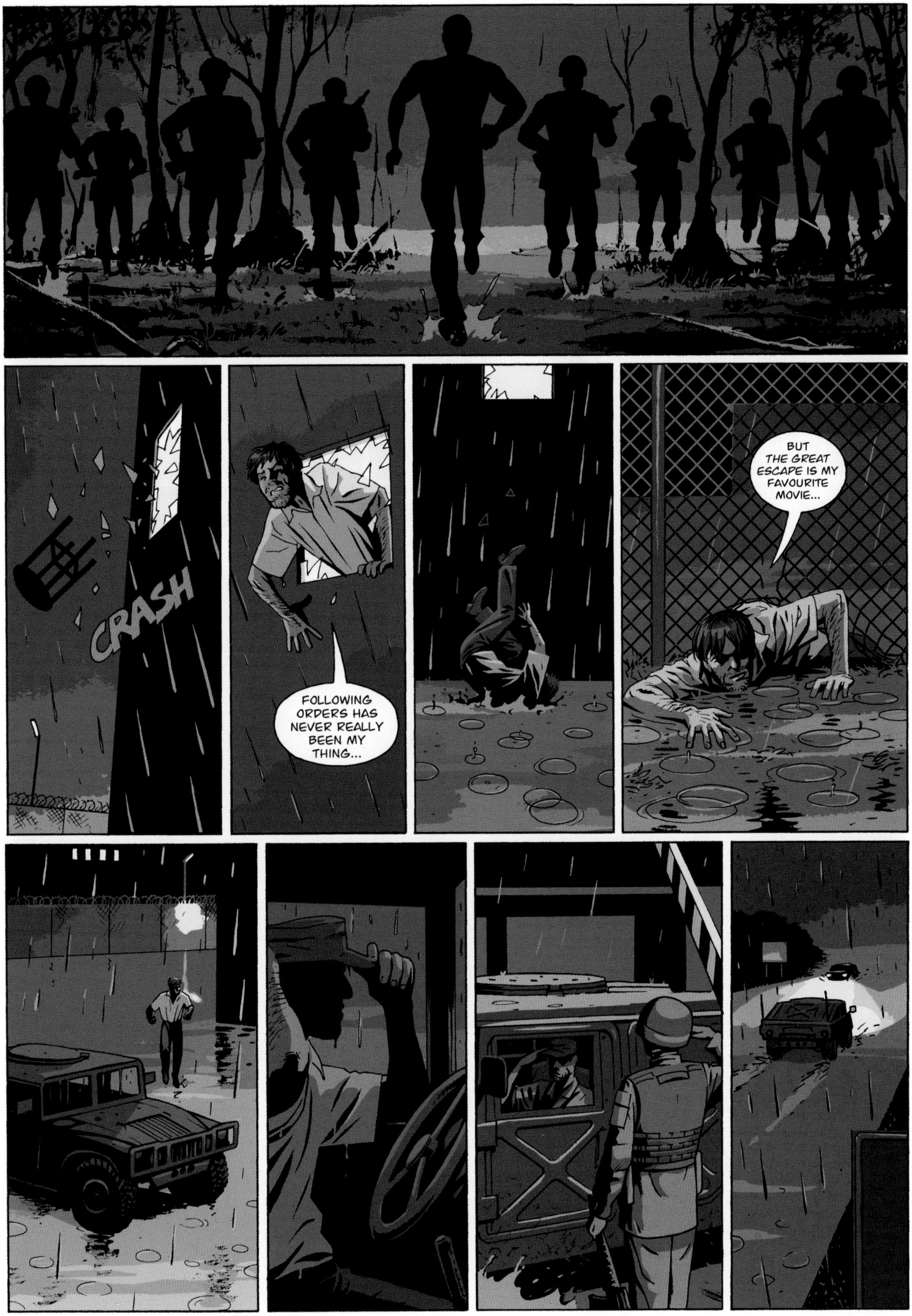
CRASH
FOLLOWING ORDERS HAS NEVER REALLY BEEN MY THING...
BUT THE GREAT ESCAPE IS MY FAVOURITE MOVIE...

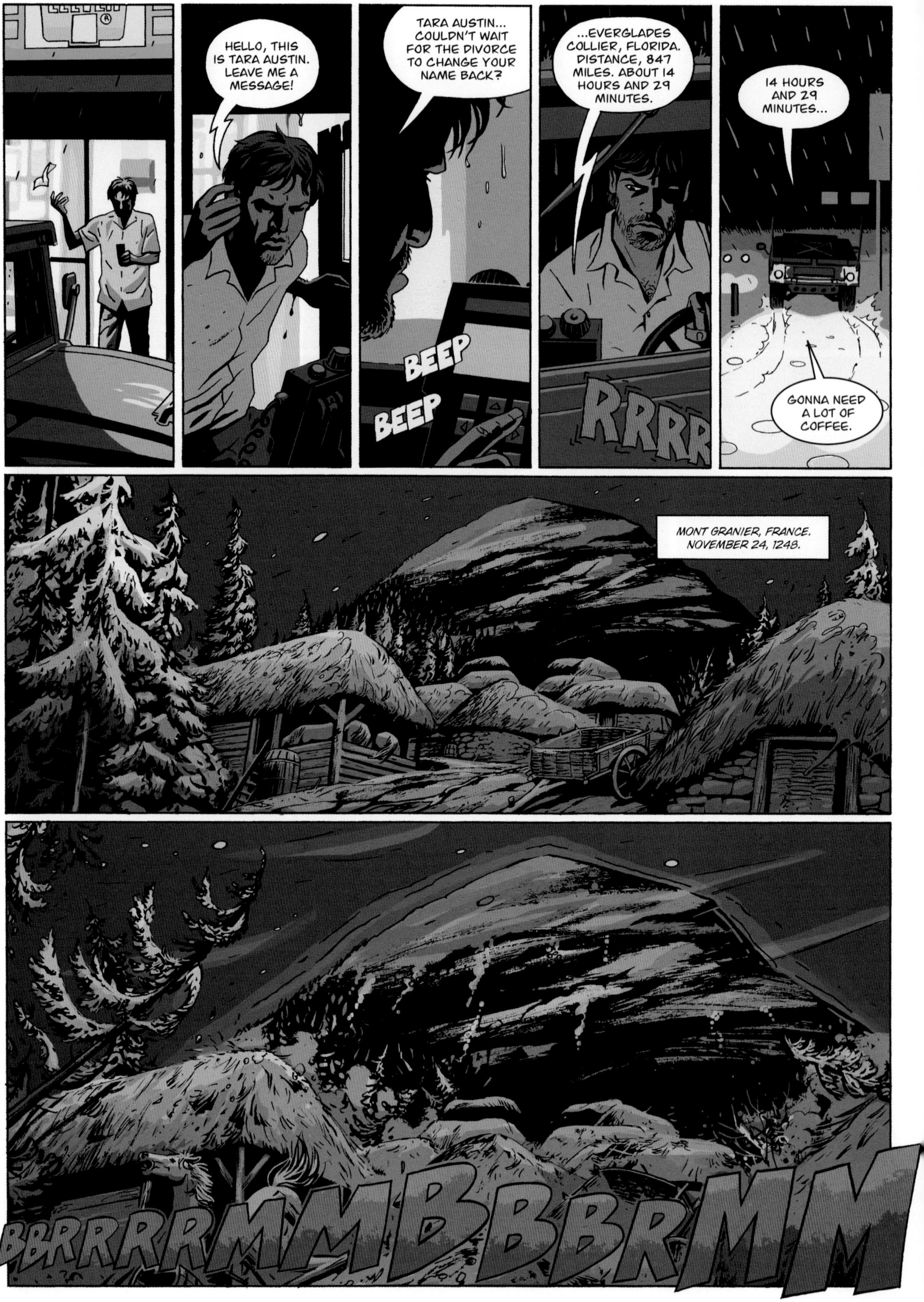
HELLO, THIS IS TARA AUSTIN. LEAVE ME A MESSAGE!
TARA AUSTIN... COULDN'T WAIT FOR THE DIVORCE TO CHANGE YOUR NAME BACK?
BEEP
BEEP
...EVERGLADES COLLIER, FLORIDA. DISTANCE, 847 MILES. ABOUT 14 HOURS AND 29 MINUTES.
RRRR
14 HOURS AND 29 MINUTES...
GONNA NEED A LOT OF COFFEE.
MONT GRANIER, FRANCE. NOVEMBER 24, 1248.
BBRRRRMMMBBBRMM

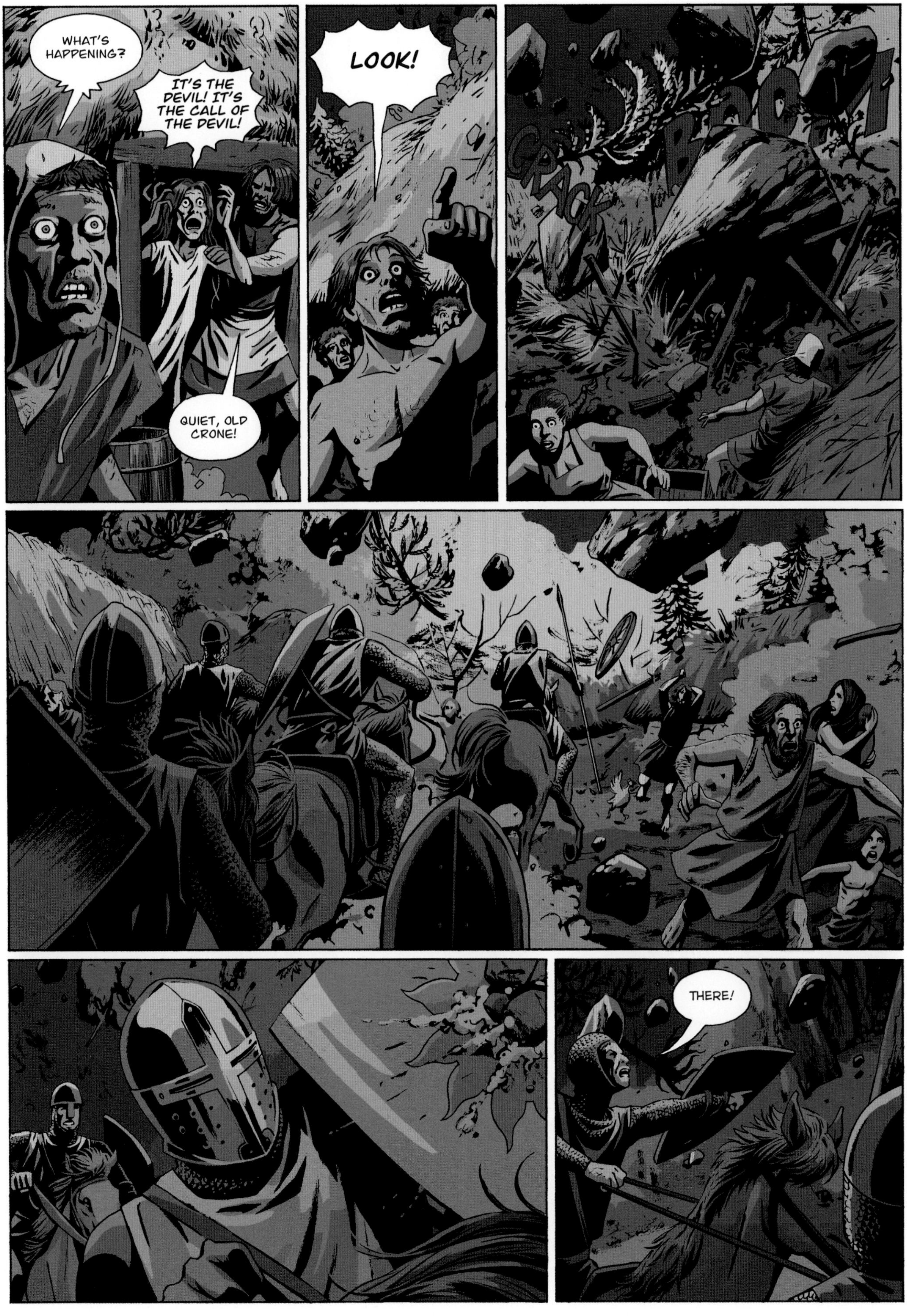
WHAT'S HAPPENING?
IT'S THE DEVIL! IT'S THE CALL OF THE DEVIL!
QUIET, OLD CRONE!
LOOK!
CRACK
BOOM
THERE!

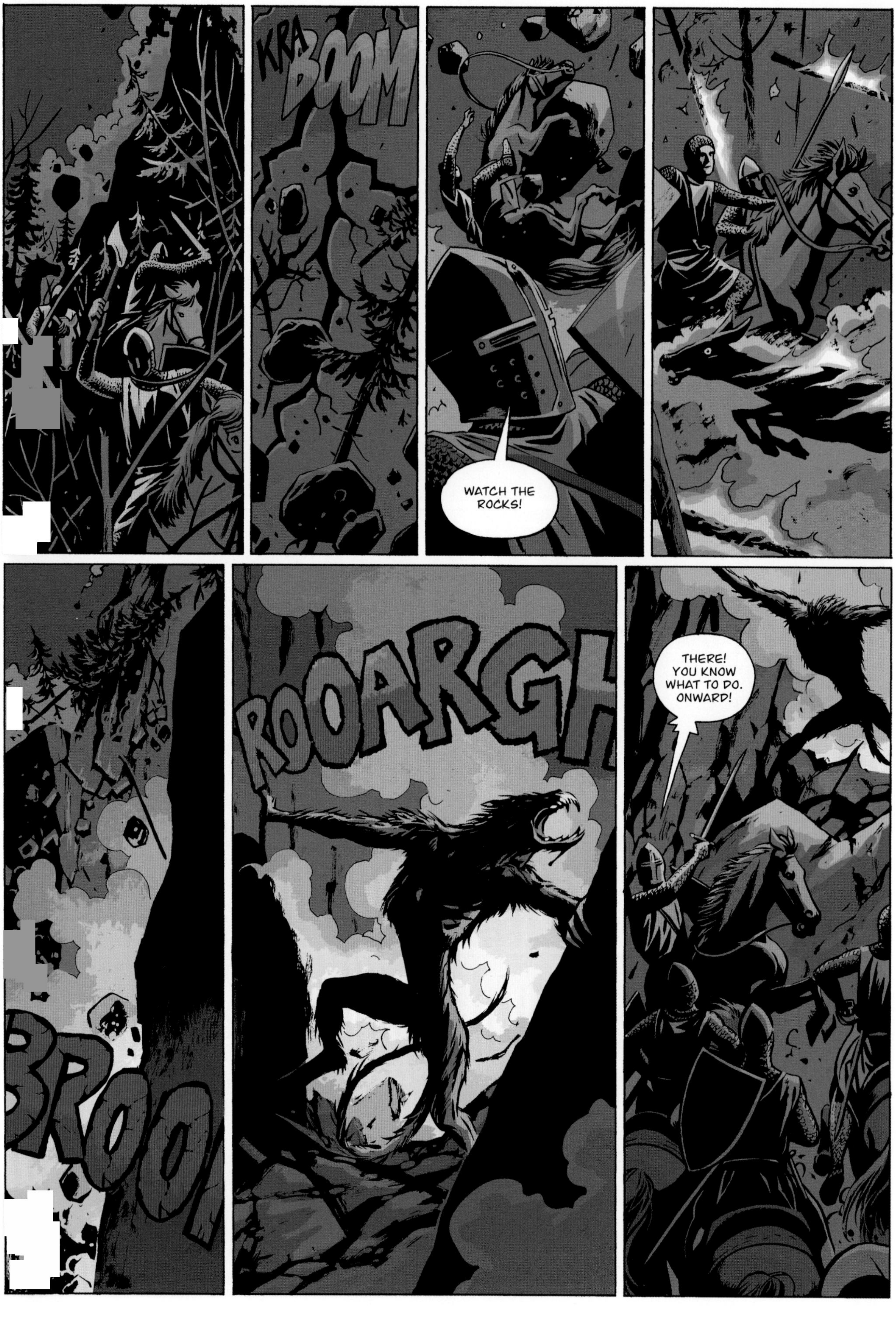
KRA BOOM
WATCH THE ROCKS!
BROOO
ROOARGH
THERE! YOU KNOW WHAT TO DO. ONWARD!

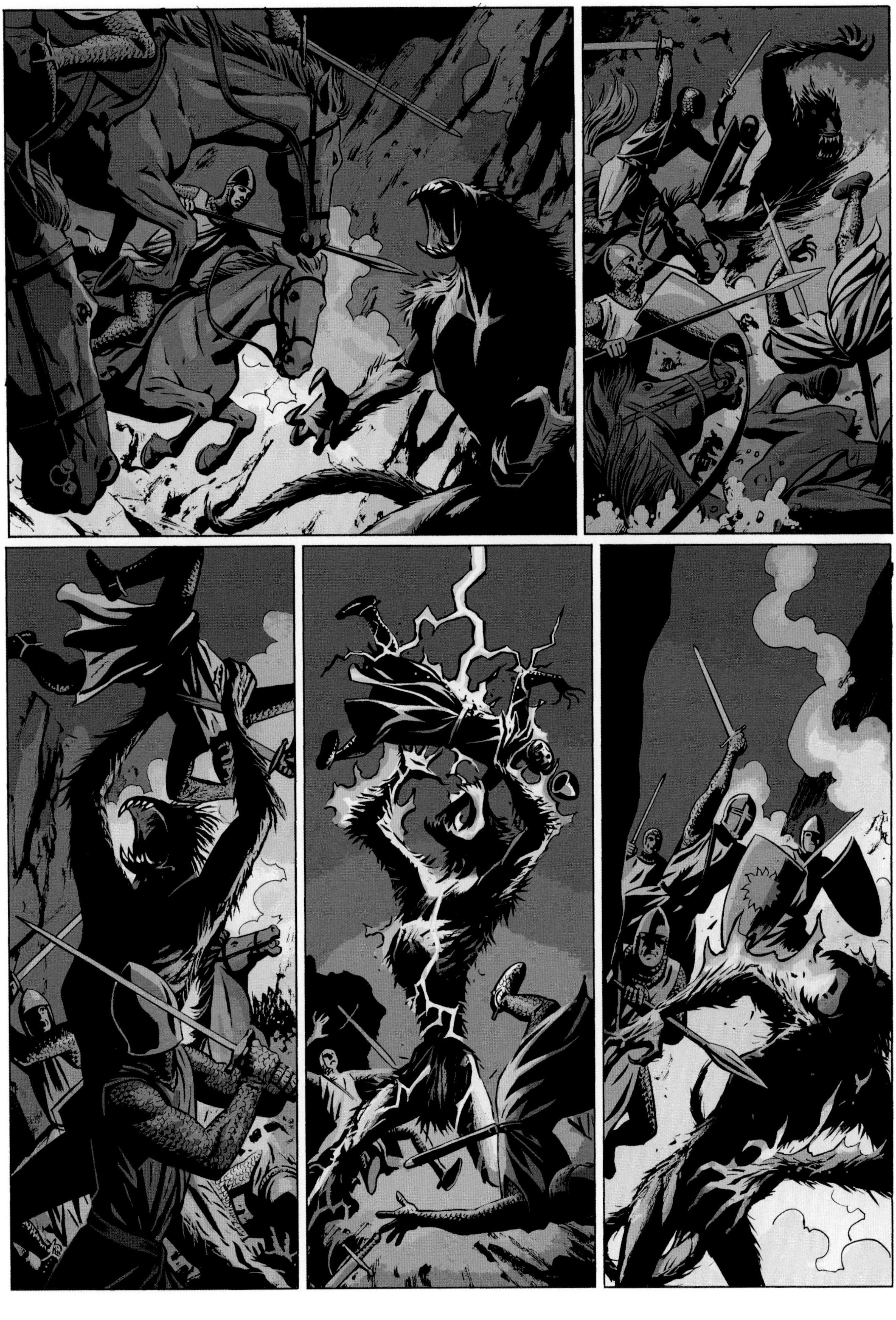

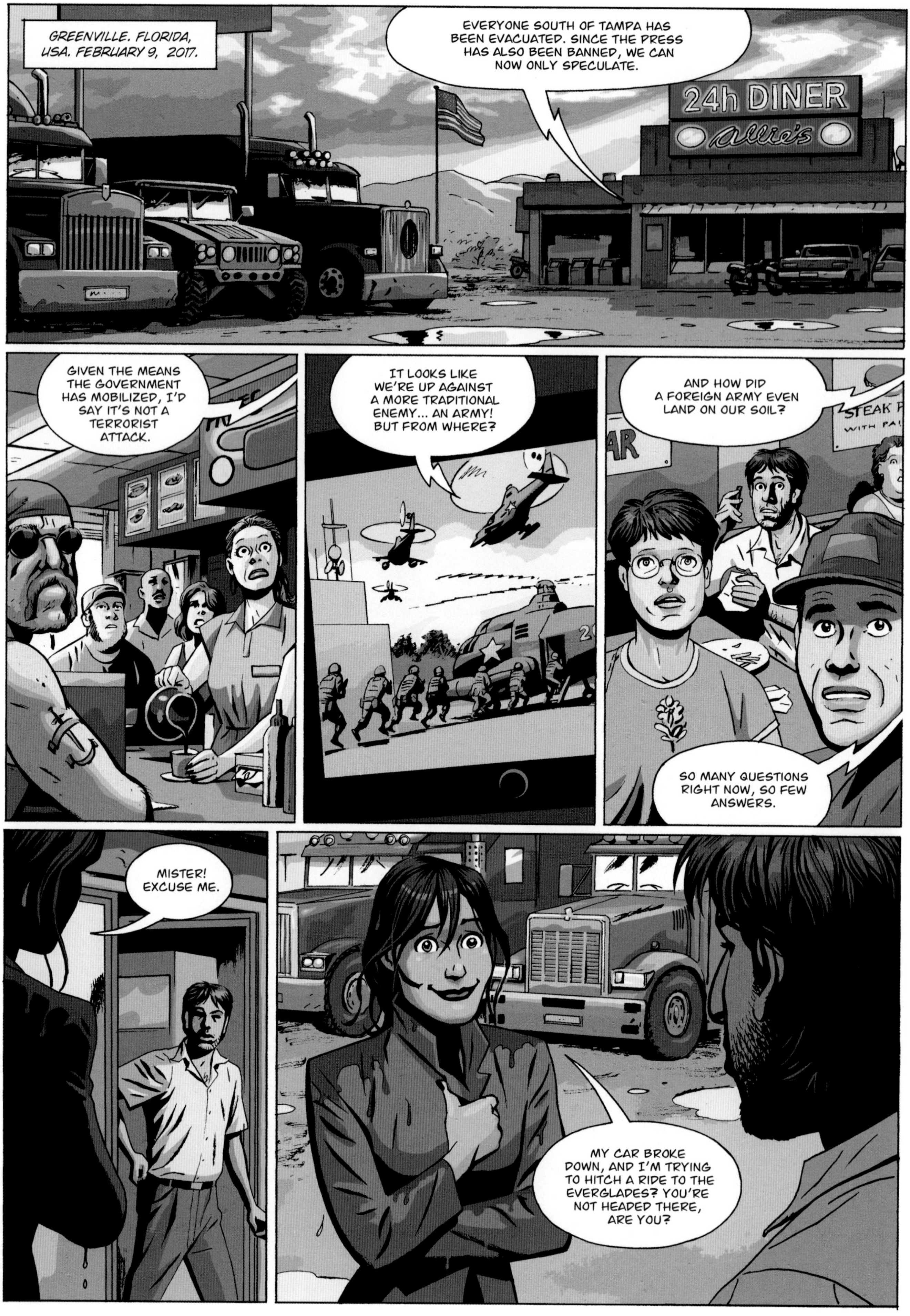
GREENVILLE. FLORIDA, USA. FEBRUARY 9, 2017.
EVERYONE SOUTH OF TAMPA HAS BEEN EVACUATED. SINCE THE PRESS HAS ALSO BEEN BANNED, WE CAN NOW ONLY SPECULATE.
24h DINER
Allie's
GIVEN THE MEANS THE GOVERNMENT HAS MOBILIZED, I'D SAY IT'S NOT A TERRORIST ATTACK.
IT LOOKS LIKE WE'RE UP AGAINST A MORE TRADITIONAL ENEMY... AN ARMY! BUT FROM WHERE?
AND HOW DID A FOREIGN ARMY EVEN LAND ON OUR SOIL?
SO MANY QUESTIONS RIGHT NOW, SO FEW ANSWERS.
MISTER! EXCUSE ME.
MY CAR BROKE DOWN, AND I'M TRYING TO HITCH A RIDE TO THE EVERGLADES? YOU'RE NOT HEADED THERE, ARE YOU?

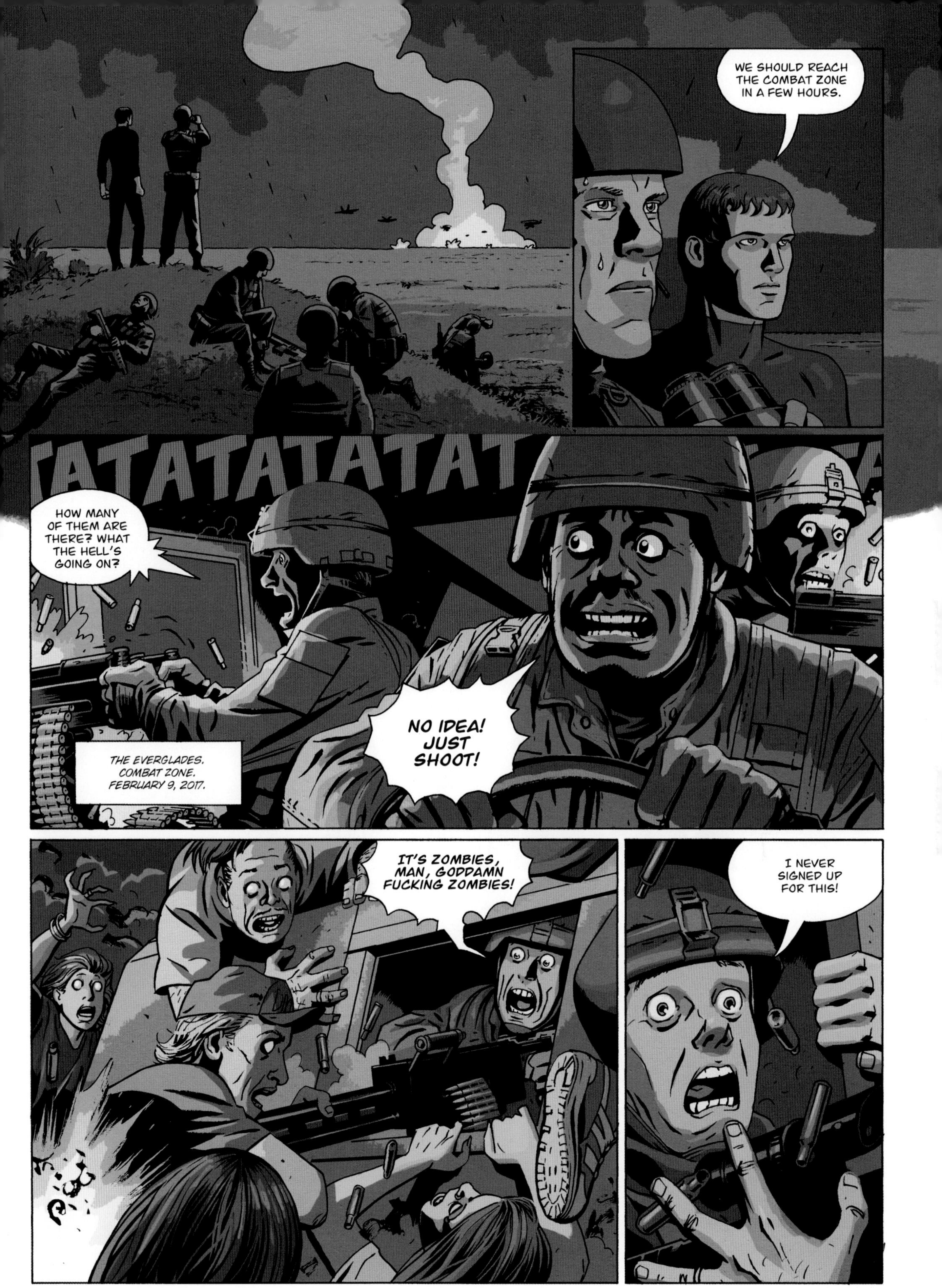
WE SHOULD REACH THE COMBAT ZONE IN A FEW HOURS.
TATATATATAT
HOW MANY OF THEM ARE THERE? WHAT THE HELL'S GOING ON?
NO IDEA! JUST SHOOT!
THE EVERGLADES. COMBAT ZONE. FEBRUARY 9, 2017.
IT'S ZOMBIES, MAN, GODDAMN FUCKING ZOMBIES!
I NEVER SIGNED UP FOR THIS!

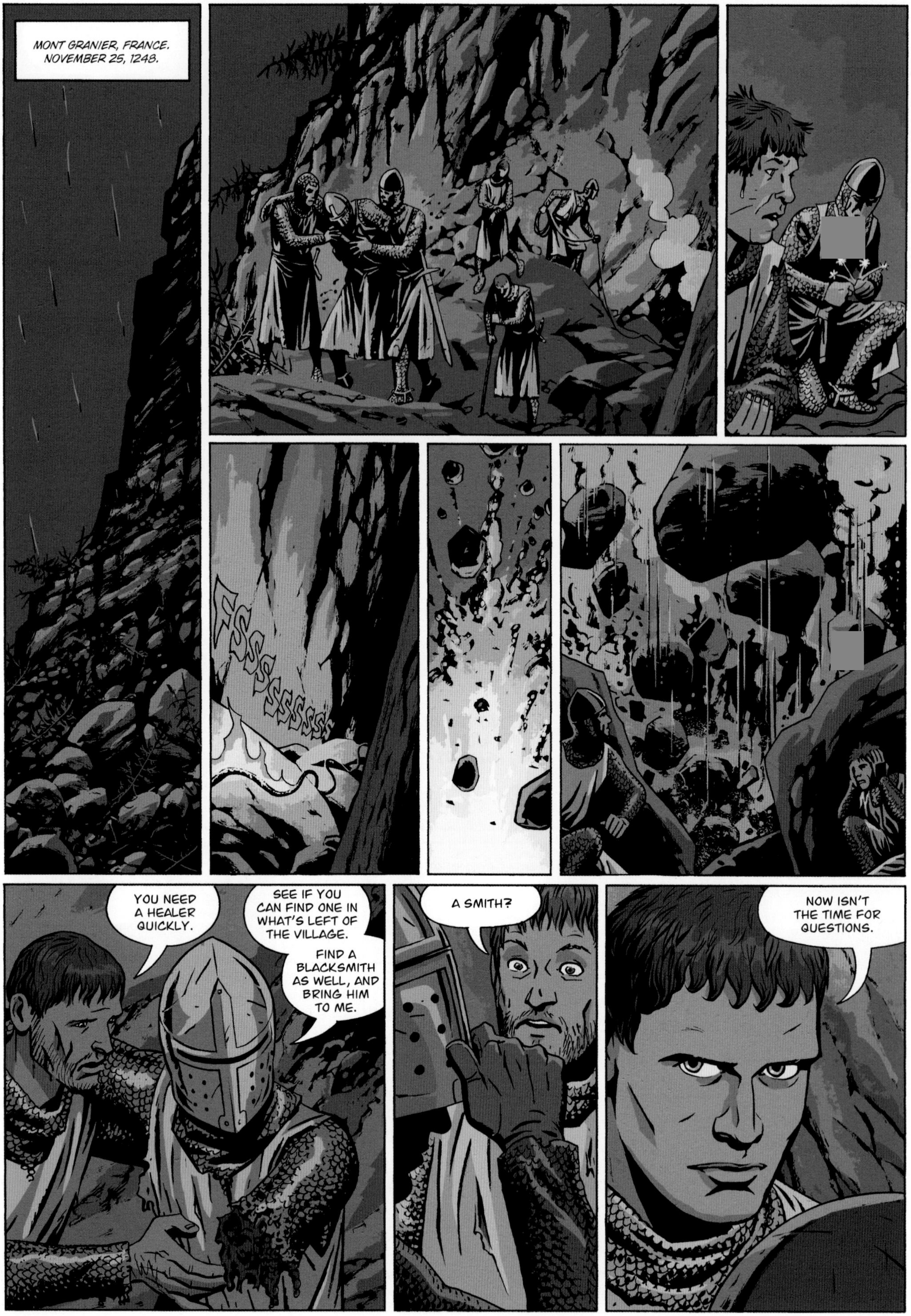
MONT GRANIER, FRANCE.
NOVEMBER 25, 1248.
FSSSSSSSSS
YOU NEED A HEALER QUICKLY.
SEE IF YOU CAN FIND ONE IN WHAT'S LEFT OF THE VILLAGE.
FIND A BLACKSMITH AS WELL, AND BRING HIM TO ME.
A SMITH?
NOW ISN'T THE TIME FOR QUESTIONS.

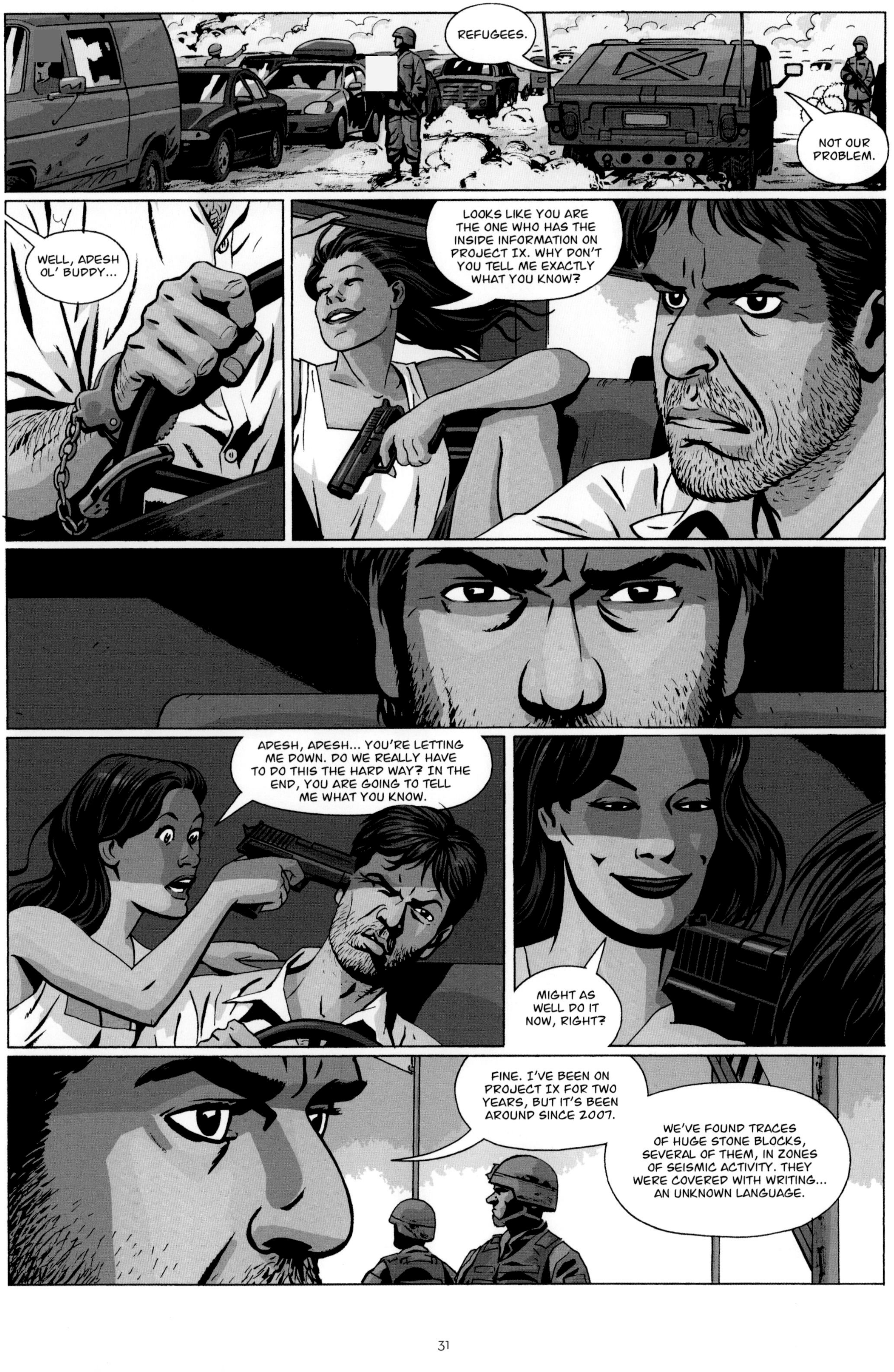
REFUGEES.
NOT OUR PROBLEM.
WELL, ADESH OL' BUDDY...
LOOKS LIKE YOU ARE THE ONE WHO HAS THE INSIDE INFORMATION ON PROJECT IX. WHY DON'T YOU TELL ME EXACTLY WHAT YOU KNOW?
ADESH, ADESH... YOU'RE LETTING ME DOWN. DO WE REALLY HAVE TO DO THIS THE HARD WAY? IN THE END, YOU ARE GOING TO TELL ME WHAT YOU KNOW.
MIGHT AS WELL DO IT NOW, RIGHT?
FINE. I'VE BEEN ON PROJECT IX FOR TWO YEARS, BUT IT'S BEEN AROUND SINCE 2007.
WE'VE FOUND TRACES OF HUGE STONE BLOCKS, SEVERAL OF THEM, IN ZONES OF SEISMIC ACTIVITY. THEY WERE COVERED WITH WRITING... AN UNKNOWN LANGUAGE.

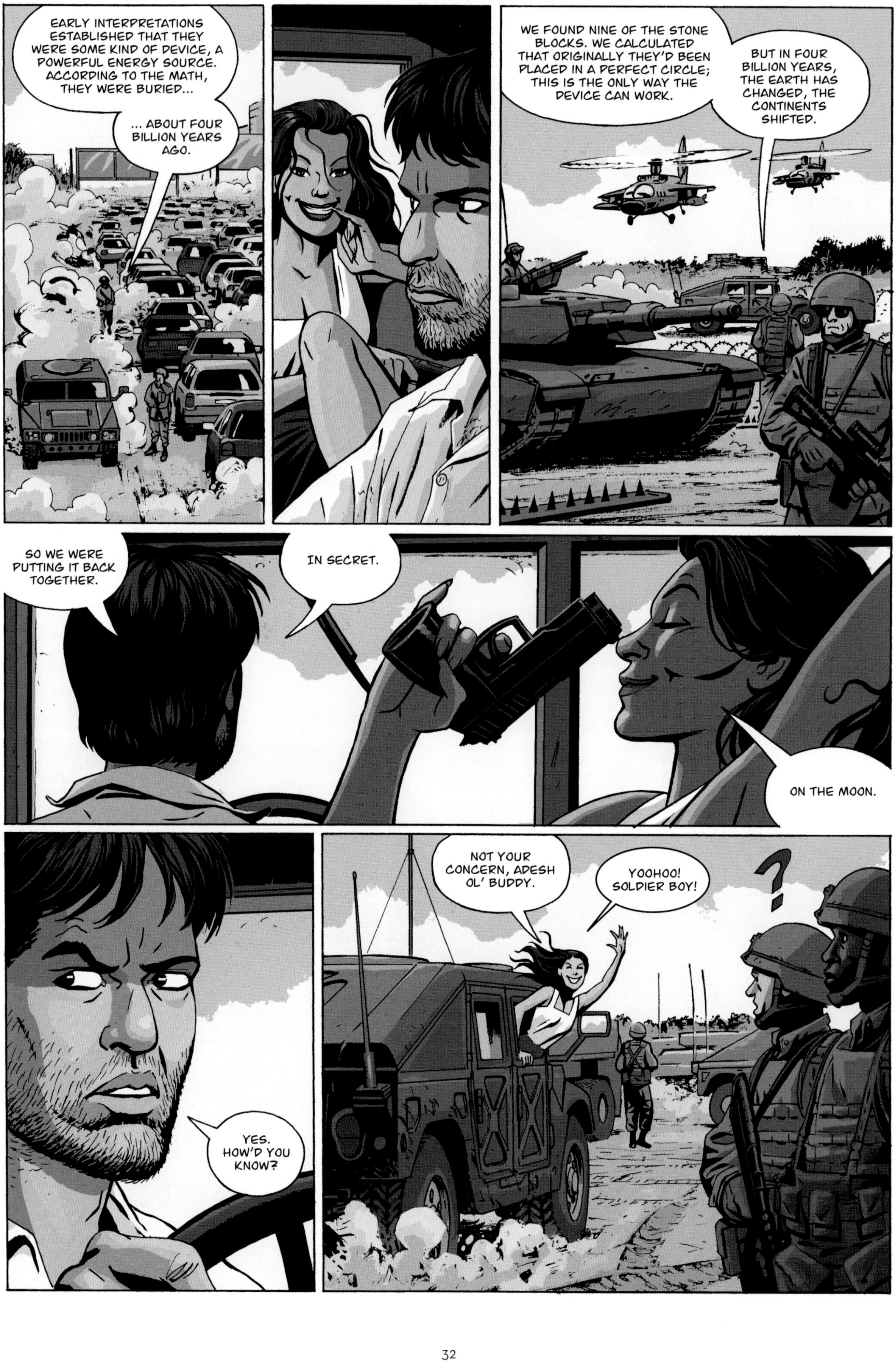
EARLY INTERPRETATIONS ESTABLISHED THAT THEY WERE SOME KIND OF DEVICE, A POWERFUL ENERGY SOURCE. ACCORDING TO THE MATH, THEY WERE BURIED...
... ABOUT FOUR BILLION YEARS AGO.
WE FOUND NINE OF THE STONE BLOCKS. WE CALCULATED THAT ORIGINALLY THEY'D BEEN PLACED IN A PERFECT CIRCLE; THIS IS THE ONLY WAY THE DEVICE CAN WORK.
BUT IN FOUR BILLION YEARS, THE EARTH HAS CHANGED, THE CONTINENTS SHIFTED.
SO WE WERE PUTTING IT BACK TOGETHER.
IN SECRET.
ON THE MOON.
YES. HOW'D YOU KNOW?
NOT YOUR CONCERN, ADESH OL' BUDDY.
YOOHOO! SOLDIER BOY!
?

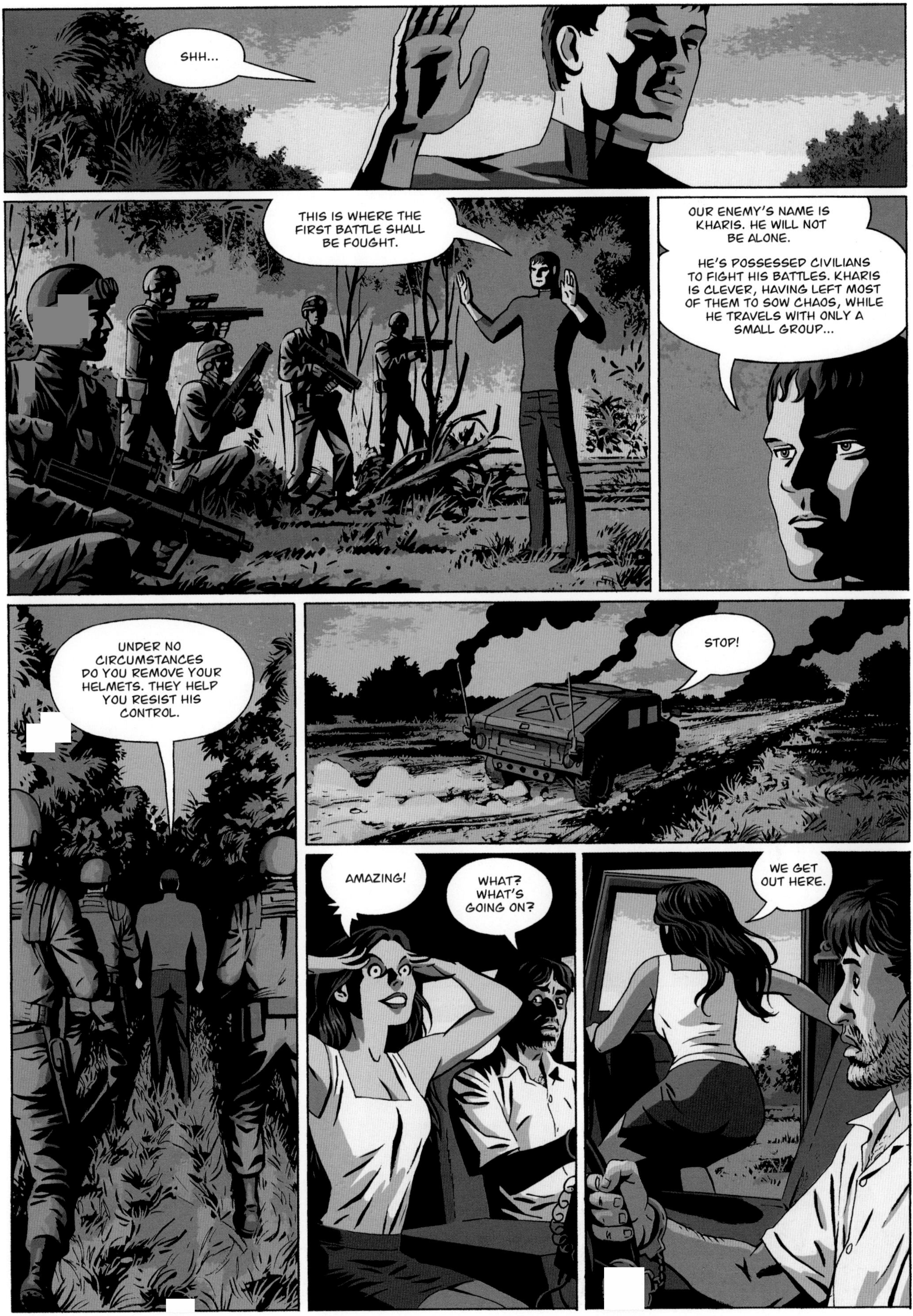
SHH...
THIS IS WHERE THE FIRST BATTLE SHALL BE FOUGHT.
OUR ENEMY'S NAME IS KHARIS. HE WILL NOT BE ALONE.
HE'S POSSESSED CIVILIANS TO FIGHT HIS BATTLES. KHARIS IS CLEVER, HAVING LEFT MOST OF THEM TO SOW CHAOS, WHILE HE TRAVELS WITH ONLY A SMALL GROUP...
UNDER NO CIRCUMSTANCES DO YOU REMOVE YOUR HELMETS. THEY HELP YOU RESIST HIS CONTROL.
STOP!
AMAZING!
WHAT? WHAT'S GOING ON?
WE GET OUT HERE.

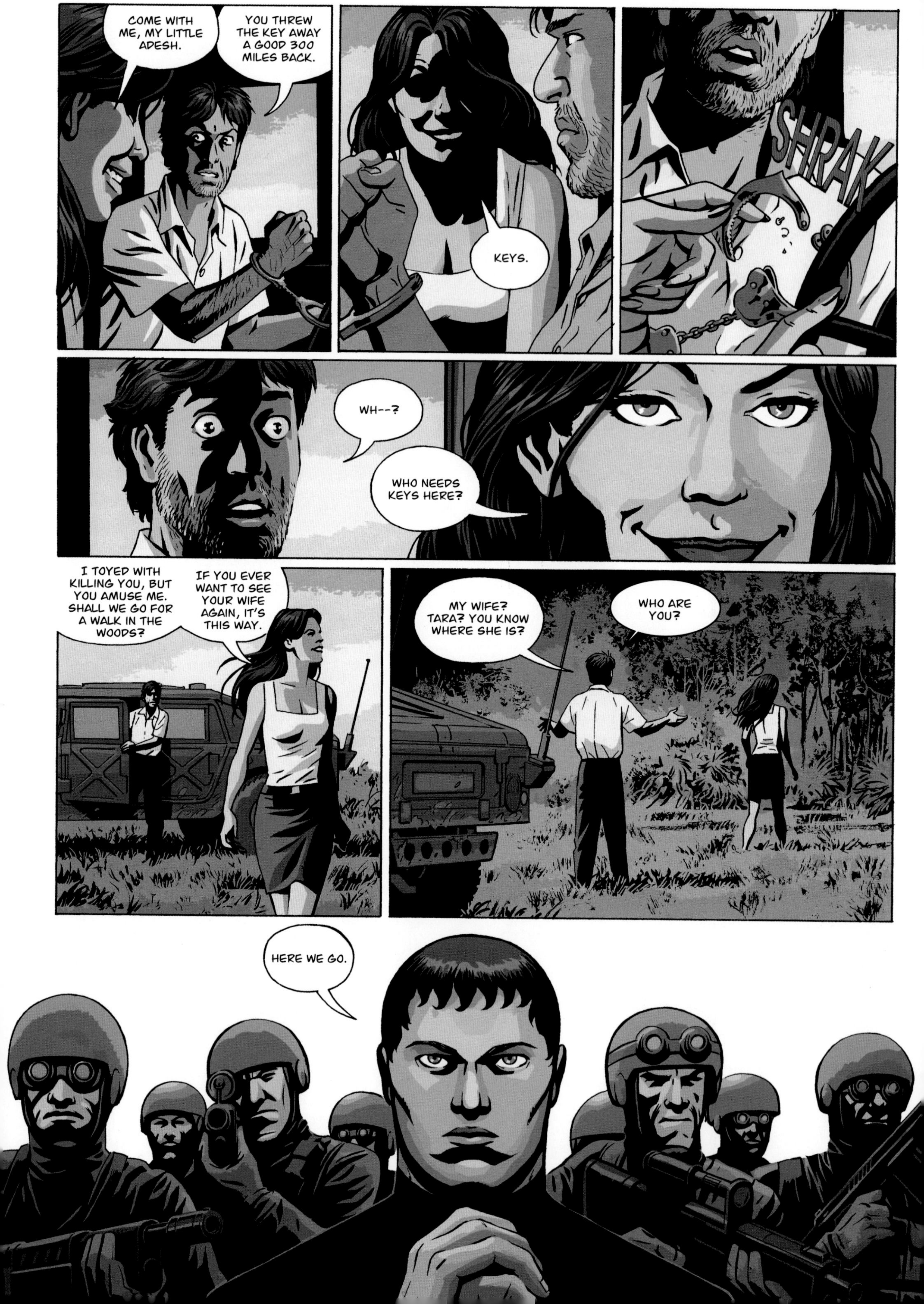
COME WITH ME, MY LITTLE ADESH.
YOU THREW THE KEY AWAY A GOOD 300 MILES BACK.
KEYS.
SHRAK
WH--?
WHO NEEDS KEYS HERE?
I TOYED WITH KILLING YOU, BUT YOU AMUSE ME. SHALL WE GO FOR A WALK IN THE WOODS?
IF YOU EVER WANT TO SEE YOUR WIFE AGAIN, IT'S THIS WAY.
MY WIFE? TARA? YOU KNOW WHERE SHE IS?
WHO ARE YOU?
HERE WE GO.

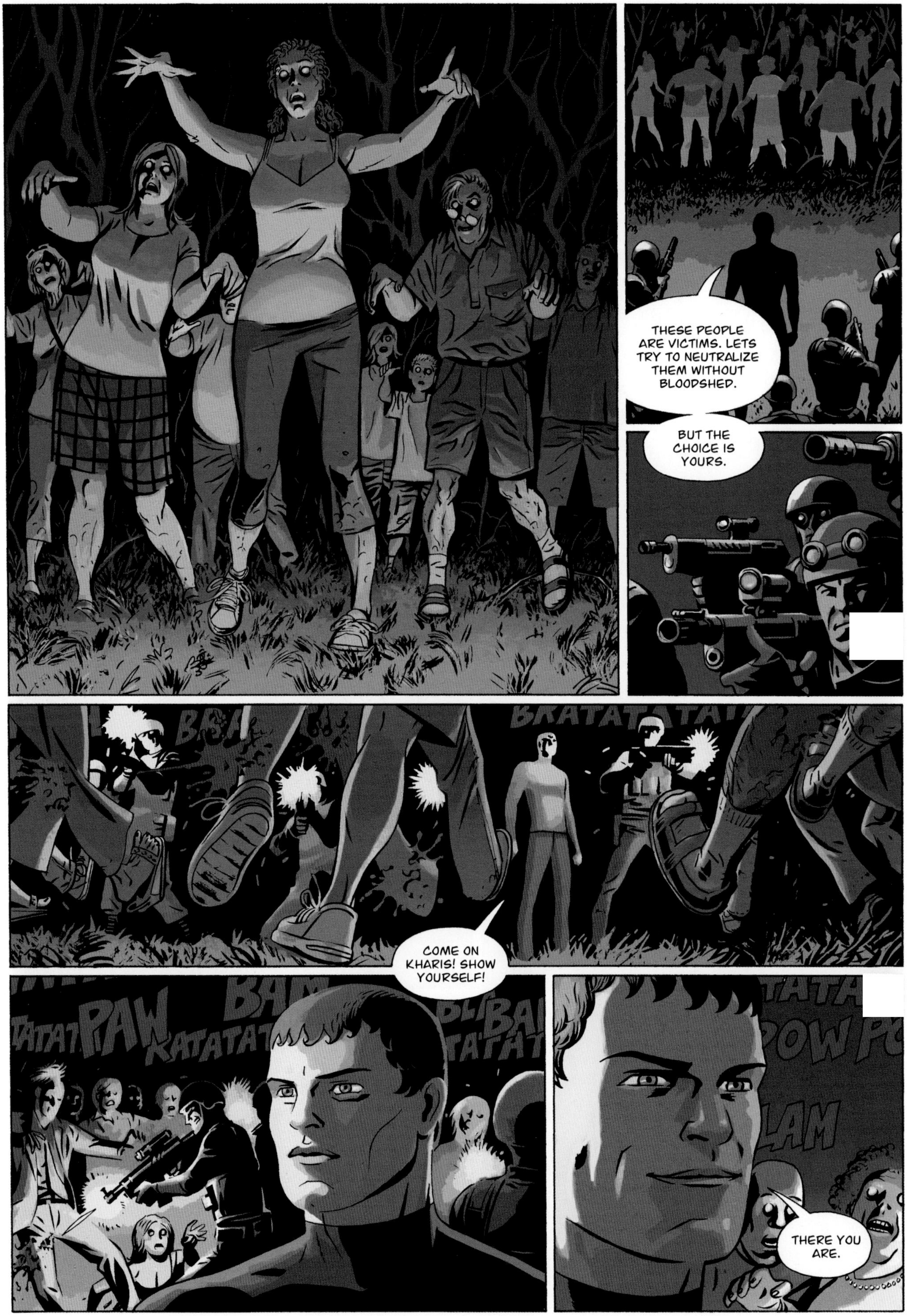
THESE PEOPLE ARE VICTIMS. LETS TRY TO NEUTRALIZE THEM WITHOUT BLOODSHED.
BUT THE CHOICE IS YOURS.
COME ON KHARIS! SHOW YOURSELF!
PAW
THERE YOU ARE.

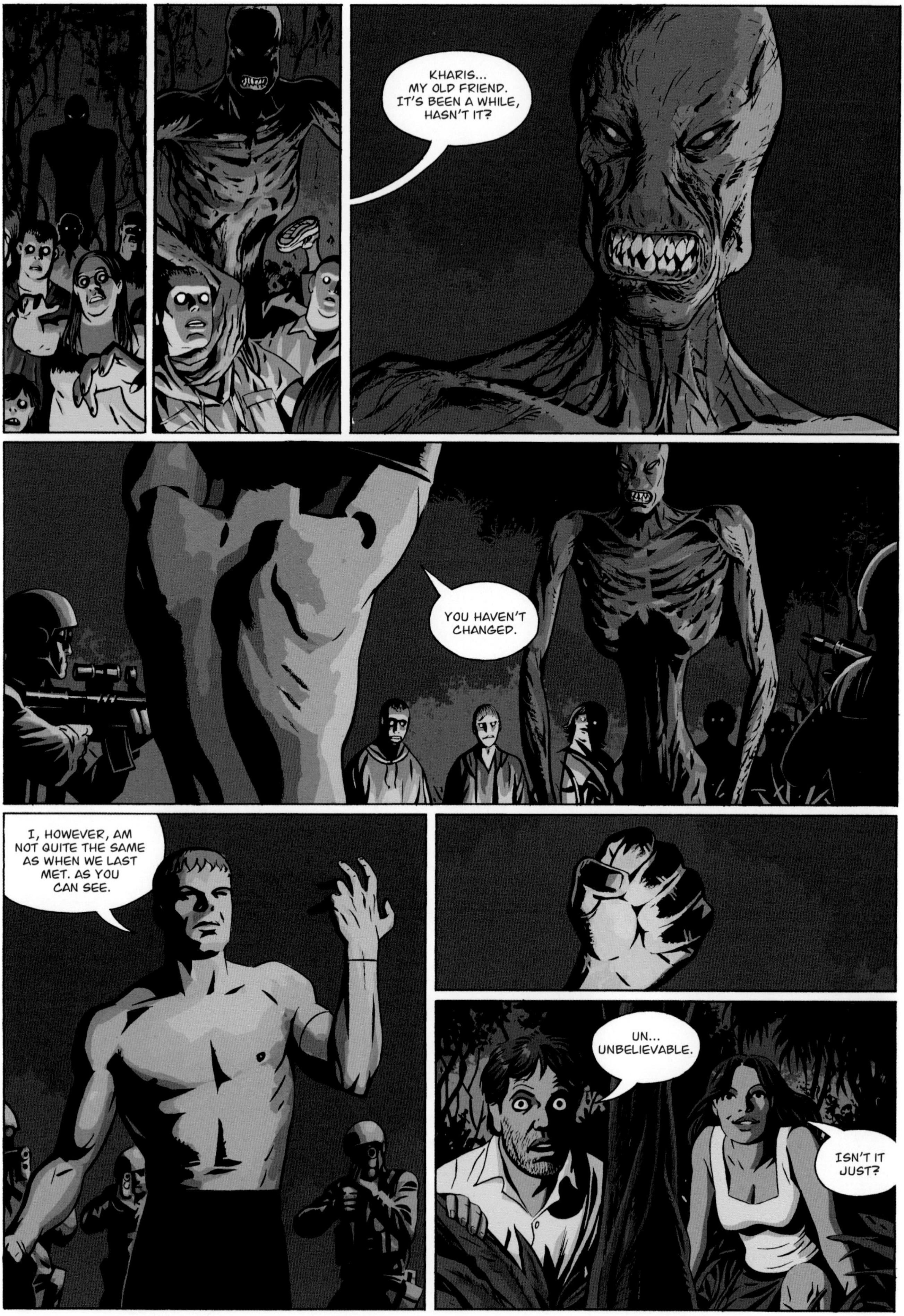
KHARIS... MY OLD FRIEND. IT'S BEEN A WHILE, HASN'T IT?
YOU HAVEN'T CHANGED.
I, HOWEVER, AM NOT QUITE THE SAME AS WHEN WE LAST MET. AS YOU CAN SEE.
UN... UNBELIEVABLE.
ISN'T IT JUST?

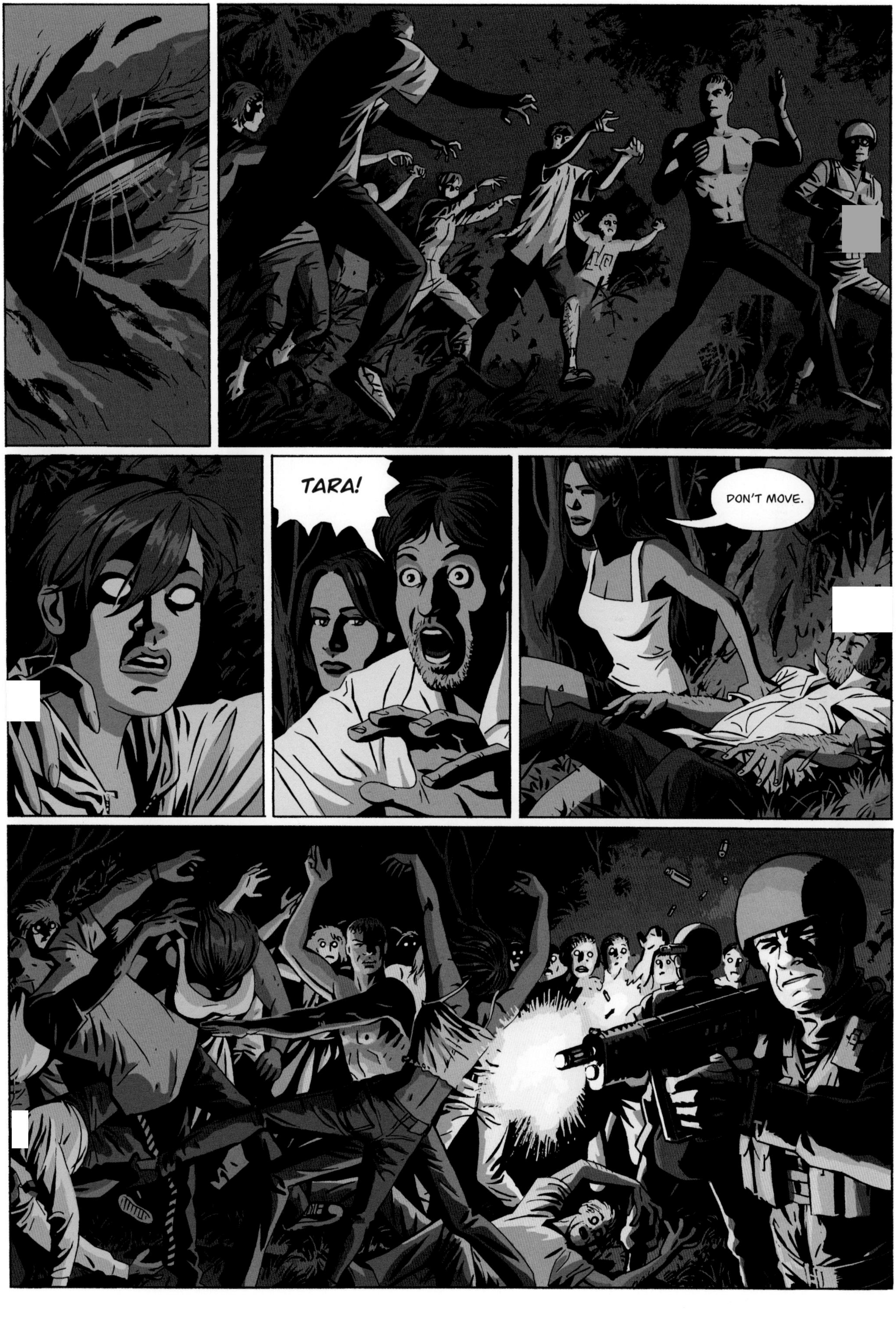
TARA!
DON'T MOVE.

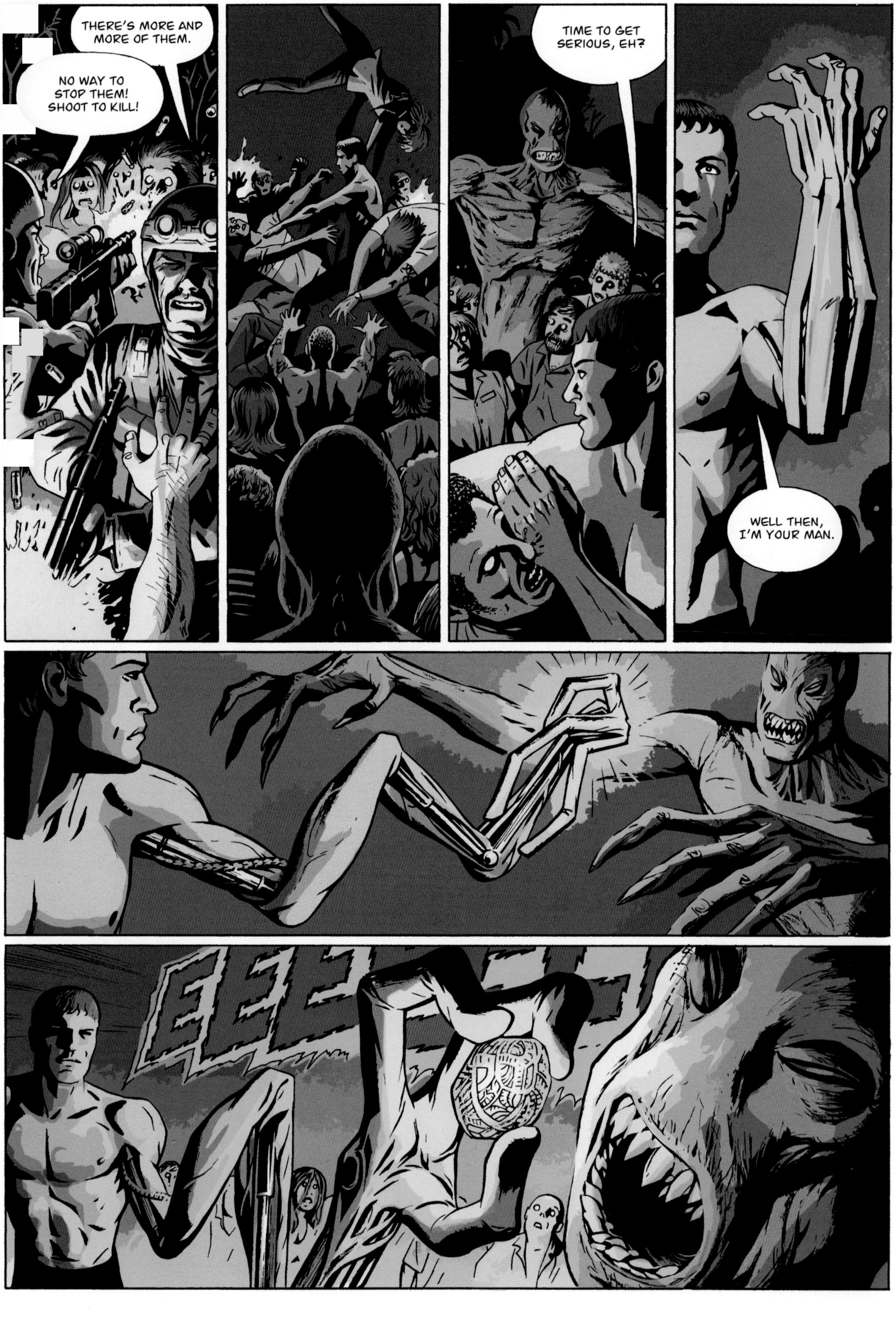
THERE'S MORE AND MORE OF THEM.
NO WAY TO STOP THEM! SHOOT TO KILL!
TIME TO GET SERIOUS, EH?
WELL THEN, I'M YOUR MAN.

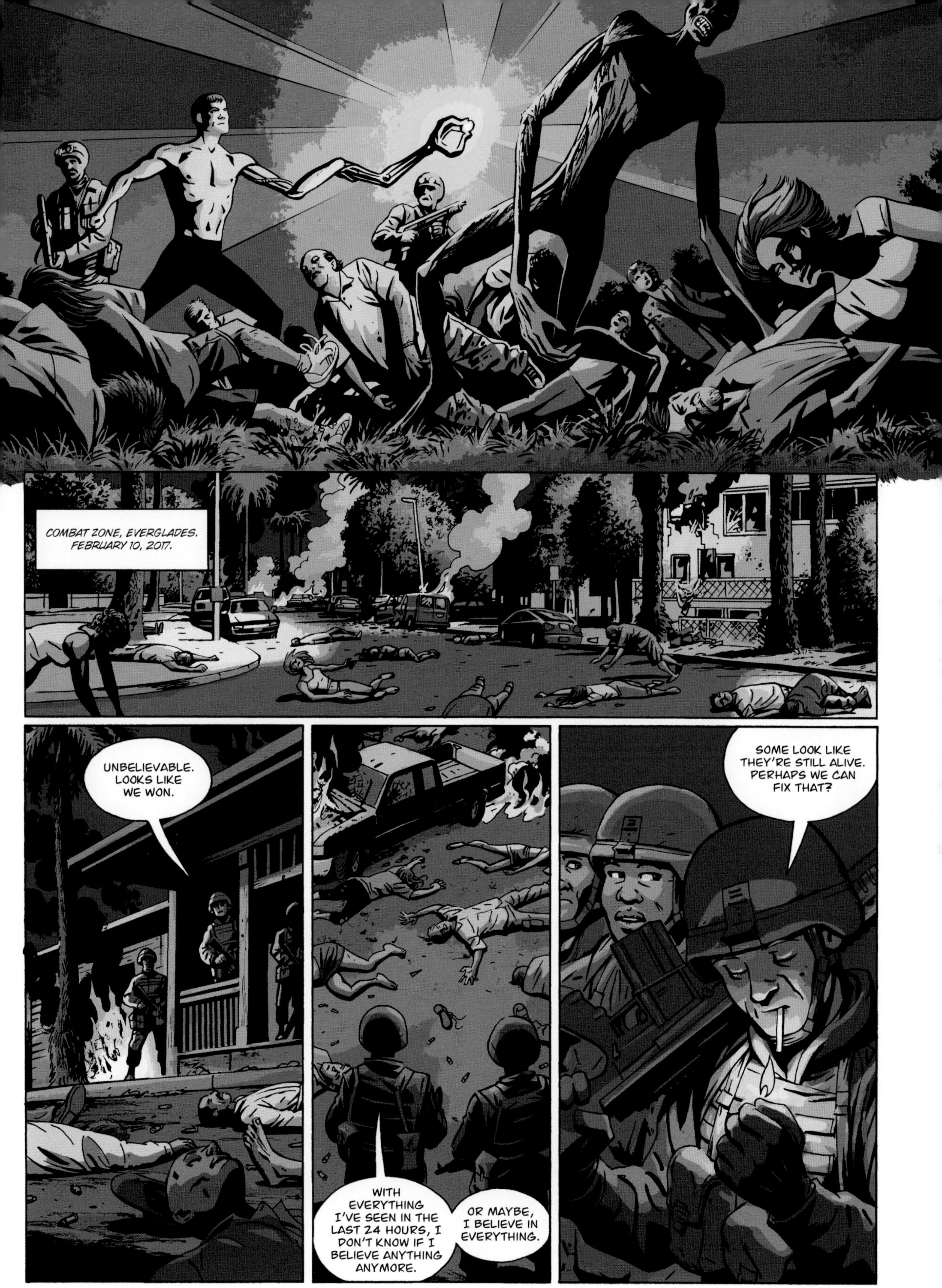
COMBAT ZONE, EVERGLADES.
FEBRUARY 10, 2017.
UNBELIEVABLE. LOOKS LIKE WE WON.
WITH EVERYTHING I'VE SEEN IN THE LAST 24 HOURS, I DON'T KNOW IF I BELIEVE ANYTHING ANYMORE.
OR MAYBE, I BELIEVE IN EVERYTHING.
SOME LOOK LIKE THEY'RE STILL ALIVE. PERHAPS WE CAN FIX THAT?

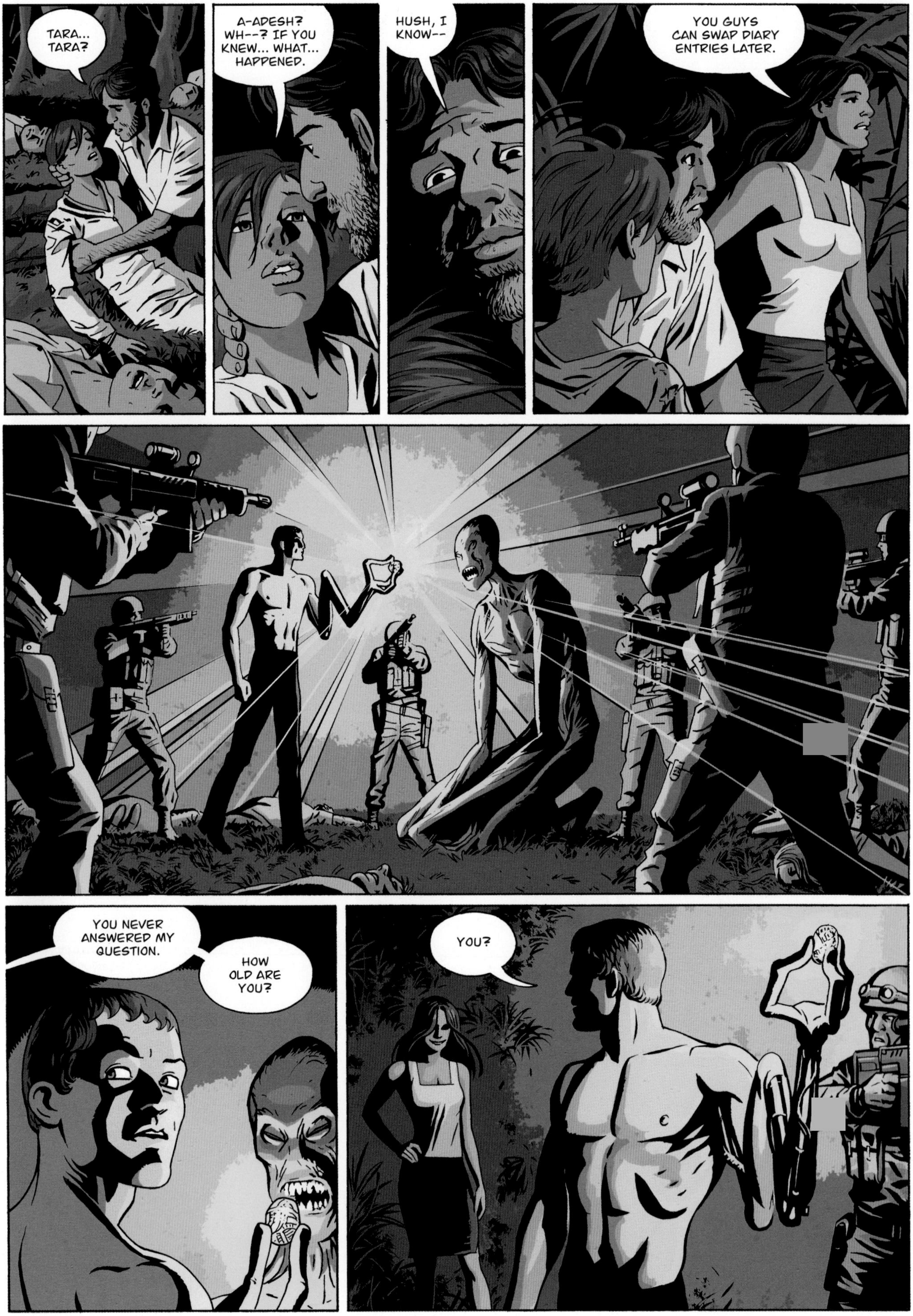
TARA... TARA?
A-ADESH? WH--? IF YOU KNEW... WHAT... HAPPENED.
HUSH, I KNOW--
YOU GUYS CAN SWAP DIARY ENTRIES LATER.
YOU NEVER ANSWERED MY QUESTION.
HOW OLD ARE YOU?
YOU?

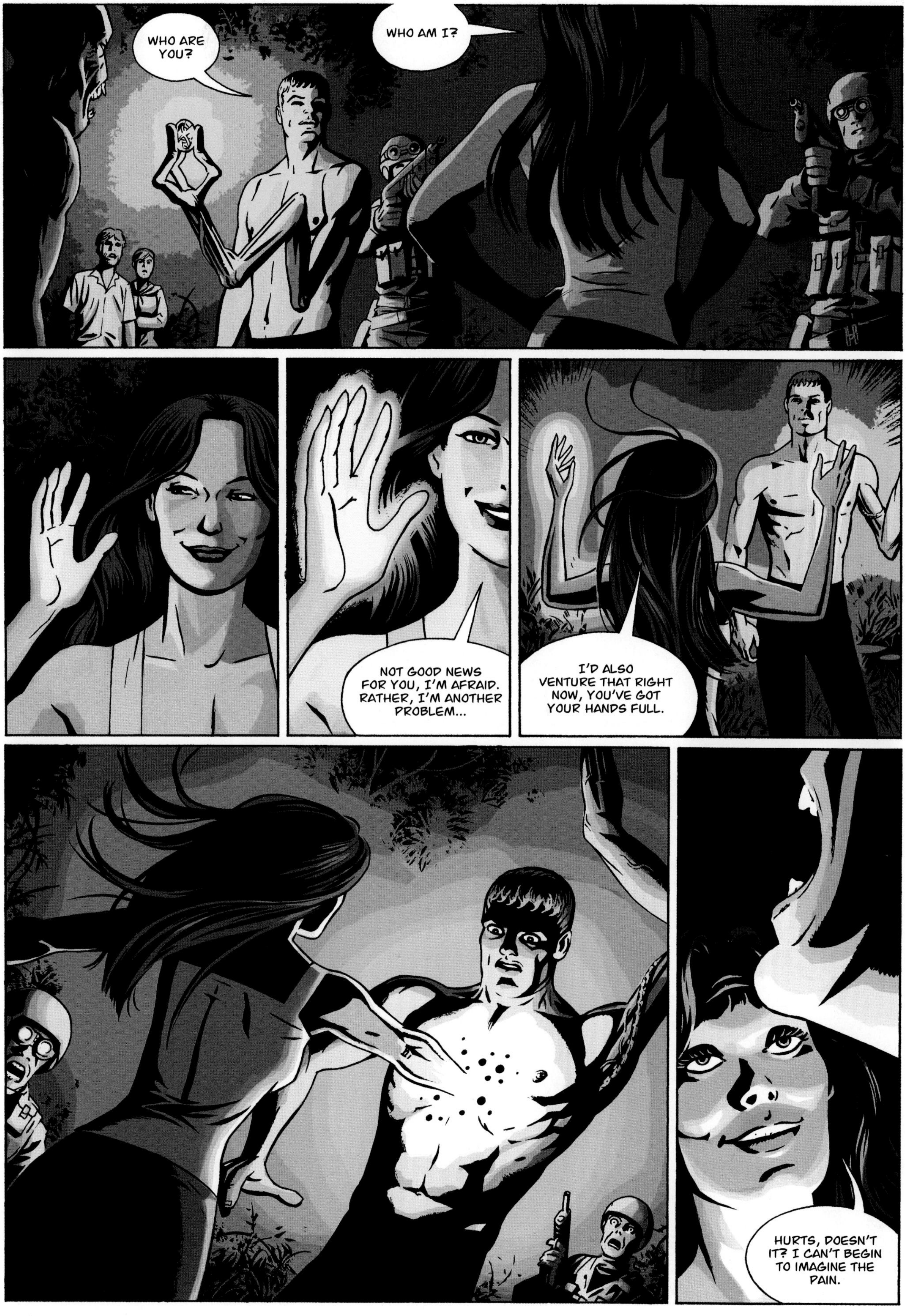
WHO ARE YOU?
WHO AM I?
NOT GOOD NEWS FOR YOU, I'M AFRAID. RATHER, I'M ANOTHER PROBLEM...
I'D ALSO VENTURE THAT RIGHT NOW, YOU'VE GOT YOUR HANDS FULL.
HURTS, DOESN'T IT? I CAN'T BEGIN TO IMAGINE THE PAIN.

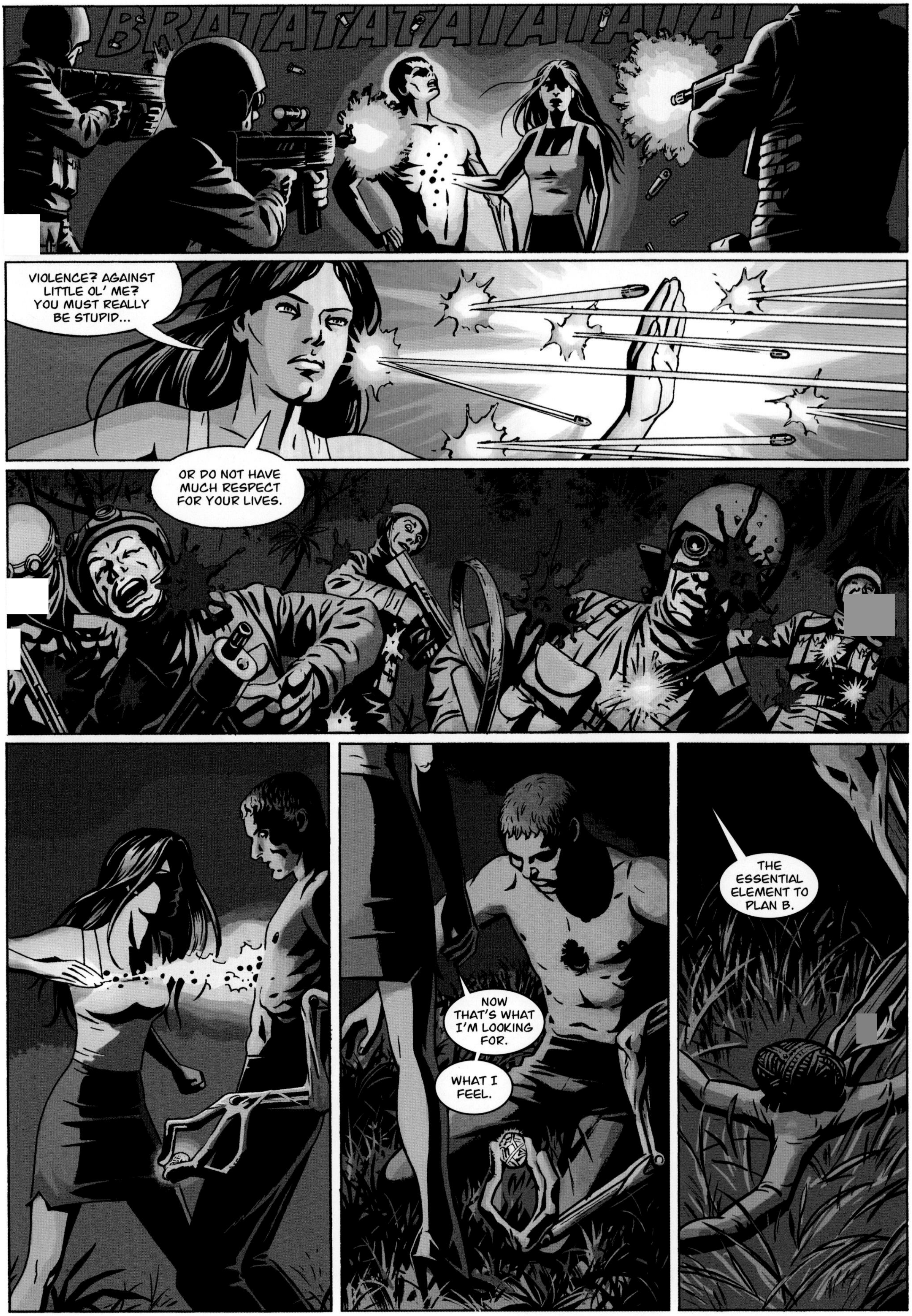
BRATATATATATATAT
VIOLENCE? AGAINST LITTLE OL' ME? YOU MUST REALLY BE STUPID...
OR DO NOT HAVE MUCH RESPECT FOR YOUR LIVES.
NOW THAT'S WHAT I'M LOOKING FOR.
WHAT I FEEL.
THE ESSENTIAL ELEMENT TO PLAN B.

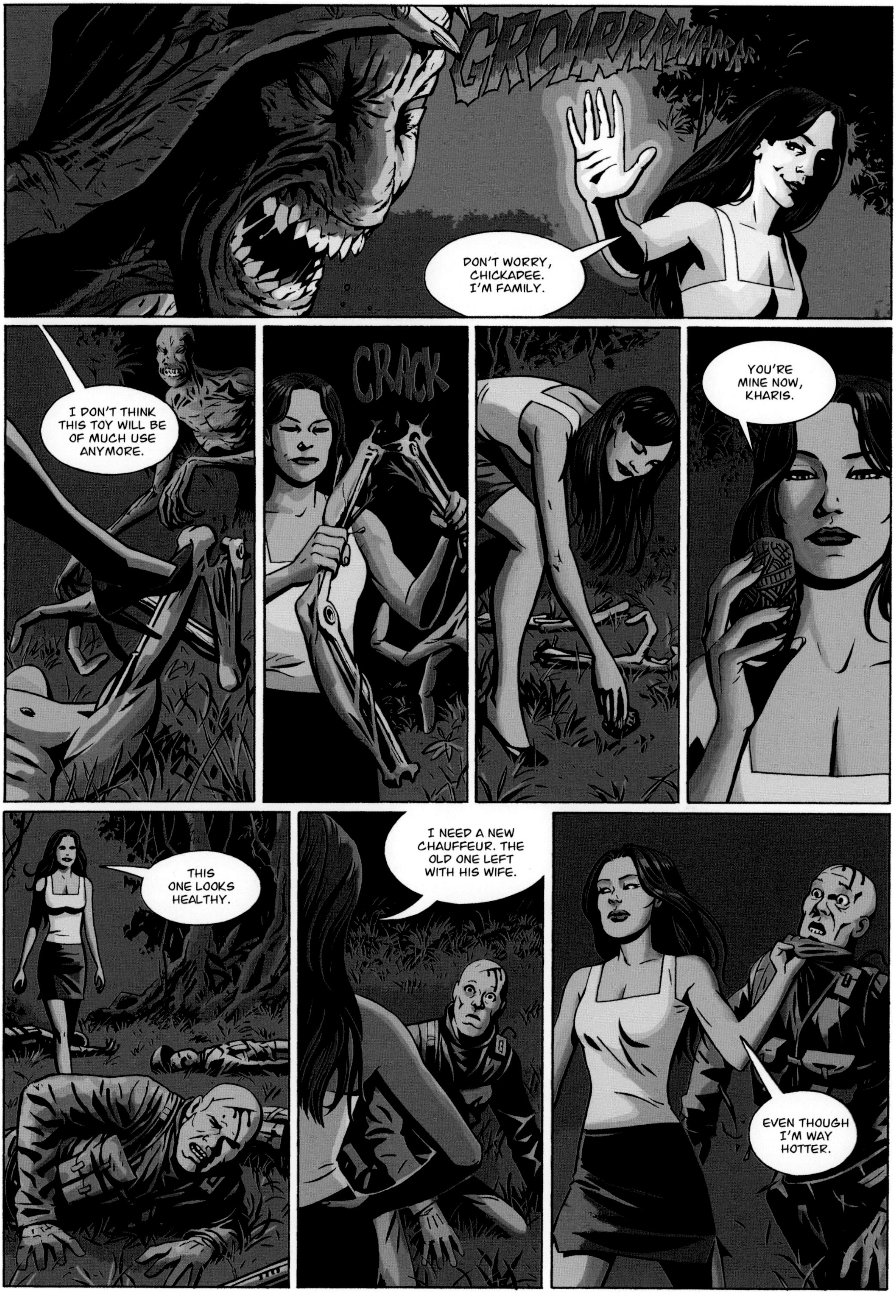
GROARRRWAARAR
DON'T WORRY, CHICKADEE. I'M FAMILY.
I DON'T THINK THIS TOY WILL BE OF MUCH USE ANYMORE.
CRACK
YOU'RE MINE NOW, KHARIS.
THIS ONE LOOKS HEALTHY.
I NEED A NEW CHAUFFEUR. THE OLD ONE LEFT WITH HIS WIFE.
EVEN THOUGH I'M WAY HOTTER.

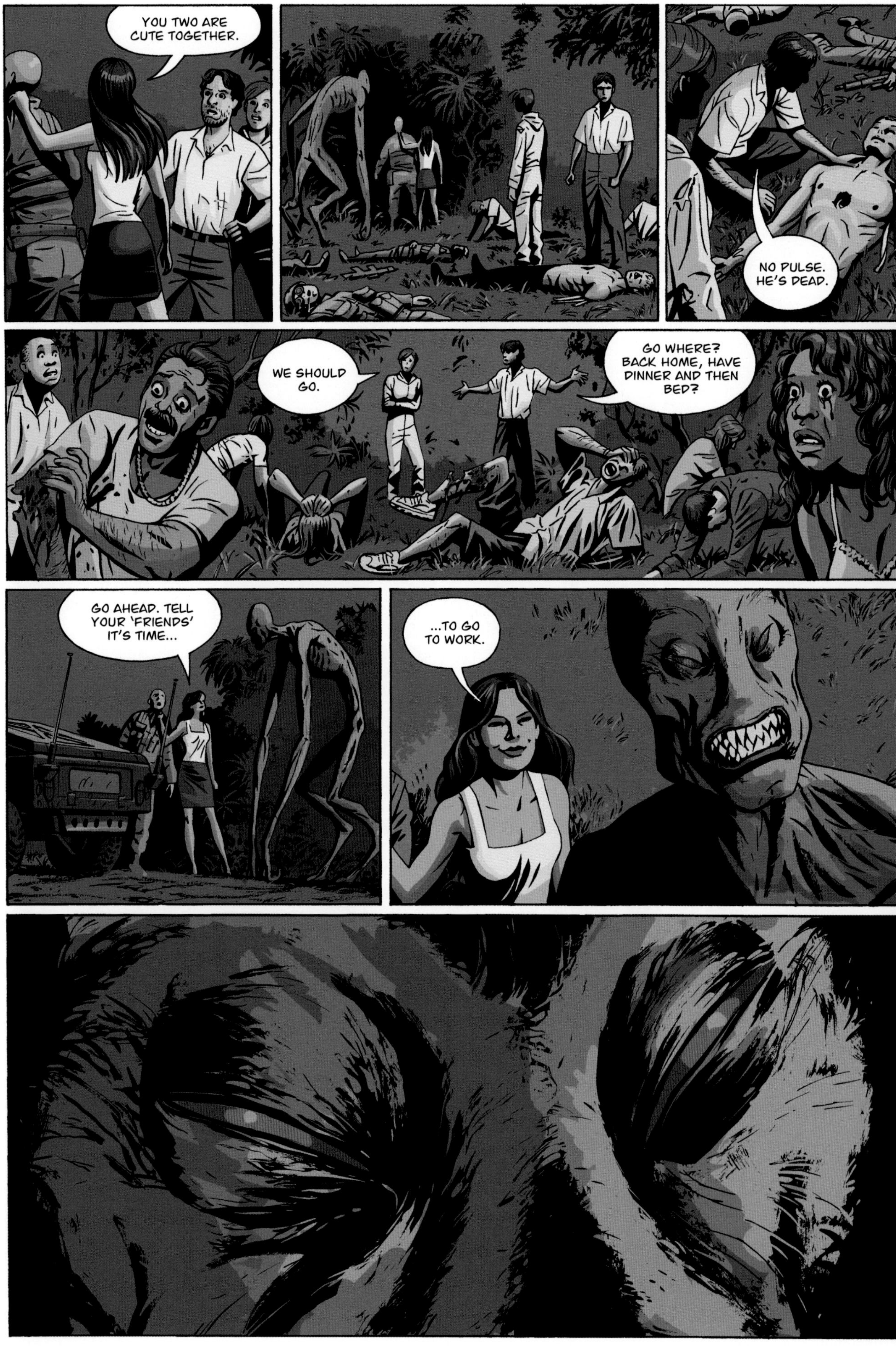
YOU TWO ARE CUTE TOGETHER.
NO PULSE. HE'S DEAD.
WE SHOULD GO.
GO WHERE? BACK HOME, HAVE DINNER AND THEN BED?
GO AHEAD. TELL YOUR 'FRIENDS' IT'S TIME...
...TO GO TO WORK.

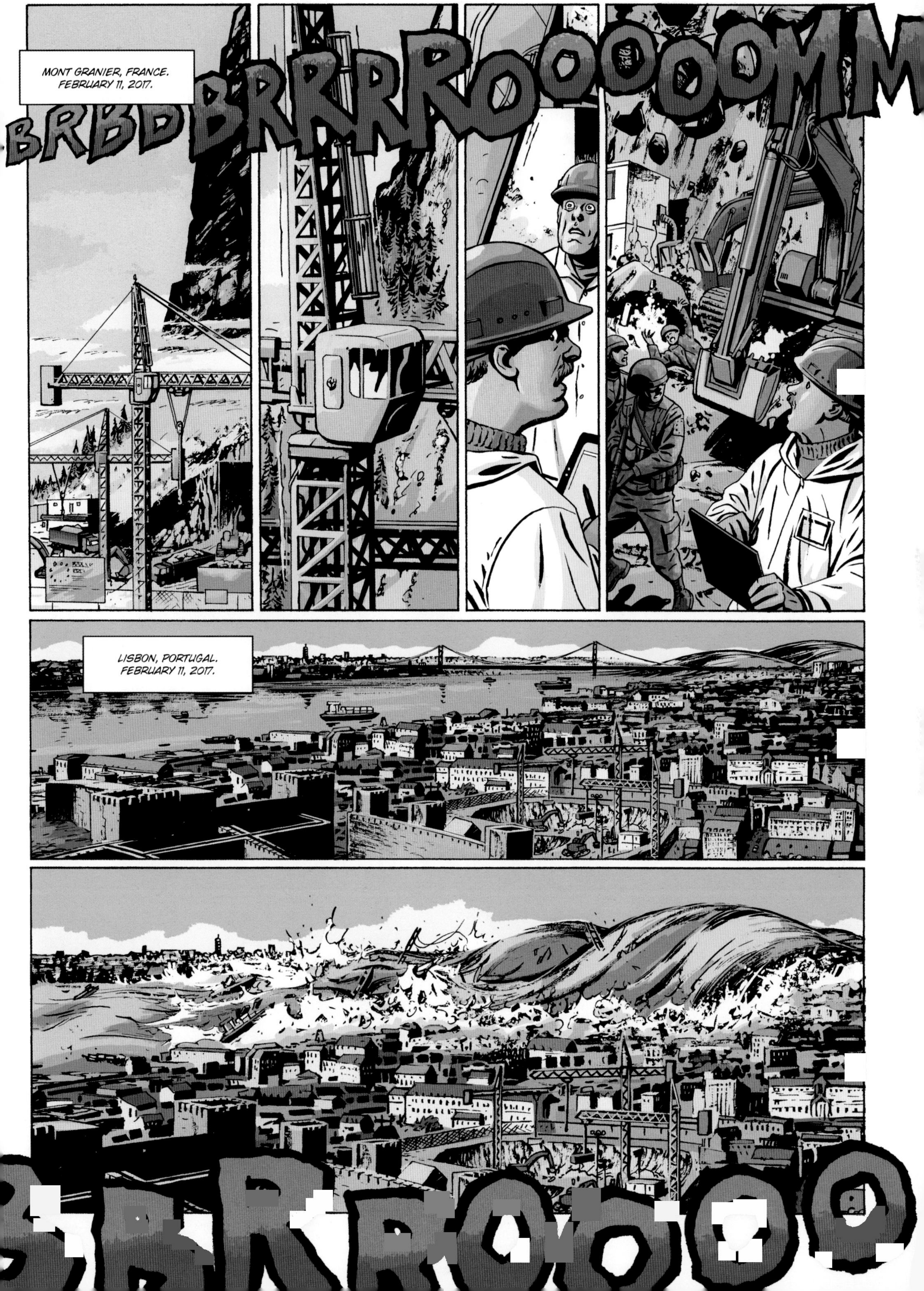
MONT GRANIER, FRANCE.
FEBRUARY 11, 2017.
BRBDBRRRROOOOOMM
LISBON, PORTUGAL.
FEBRUARY 11, 2017.

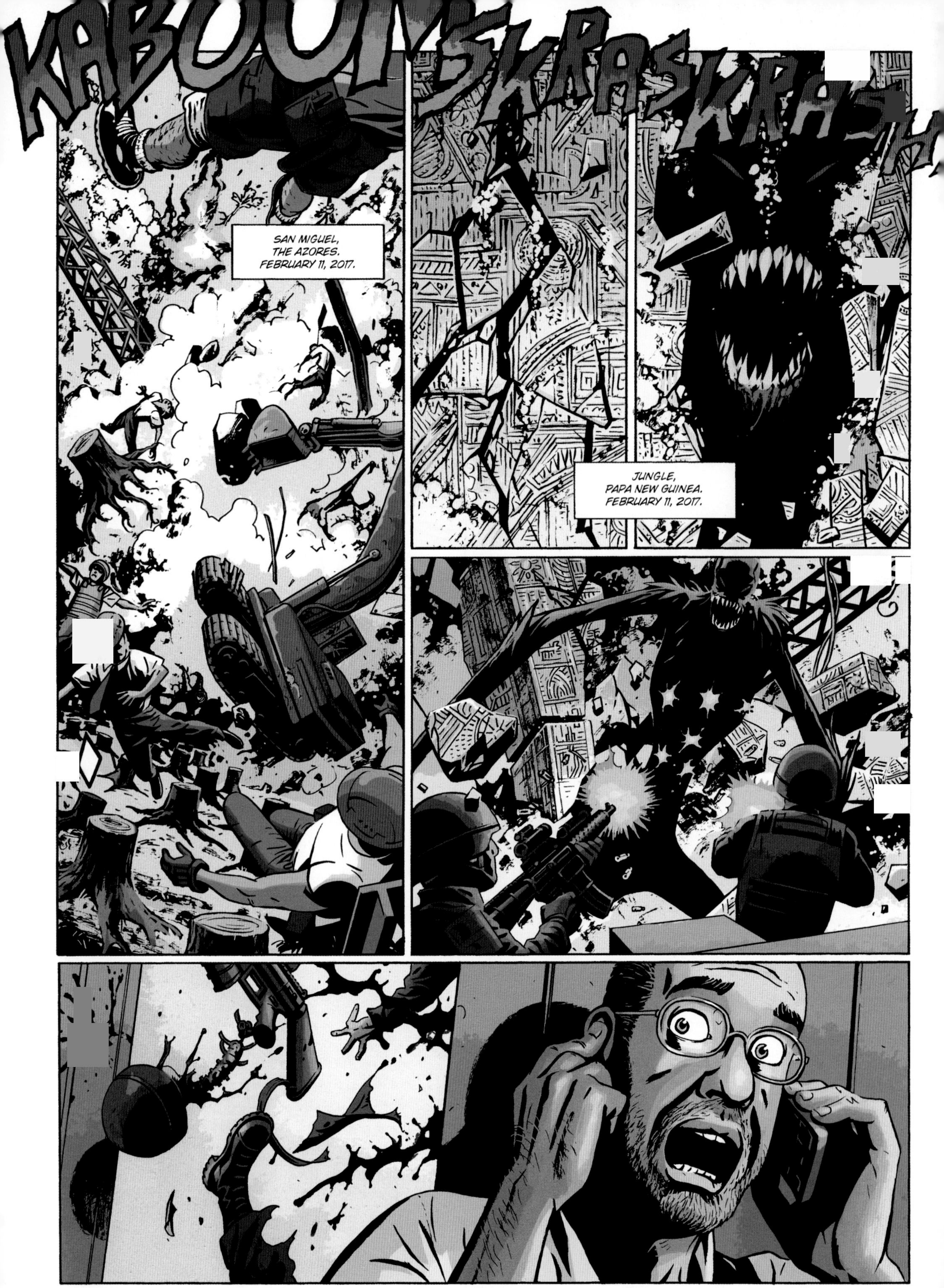
KABOOM
SKRASKRASH
SAN MIGUEL, THE AZORES. FEBRUARY 11, 2017.
JUNGLE, PAPA NEW GUINEA. FEBRUARY 11, 2017.

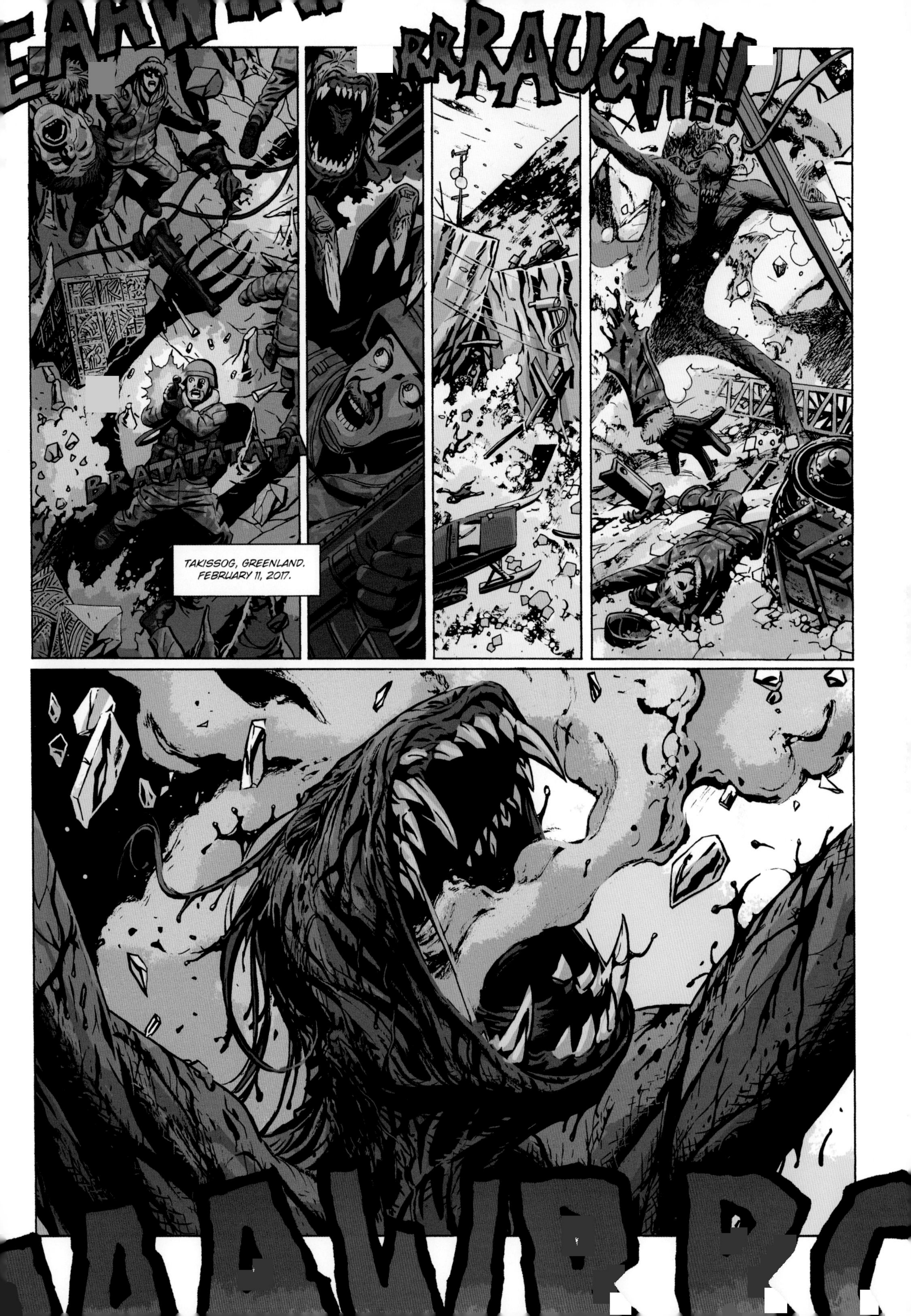
RRRAUGH!!
BRATATATATA
TAKISSOG, GREENLAND.
FEBRUARY 11, 2017.

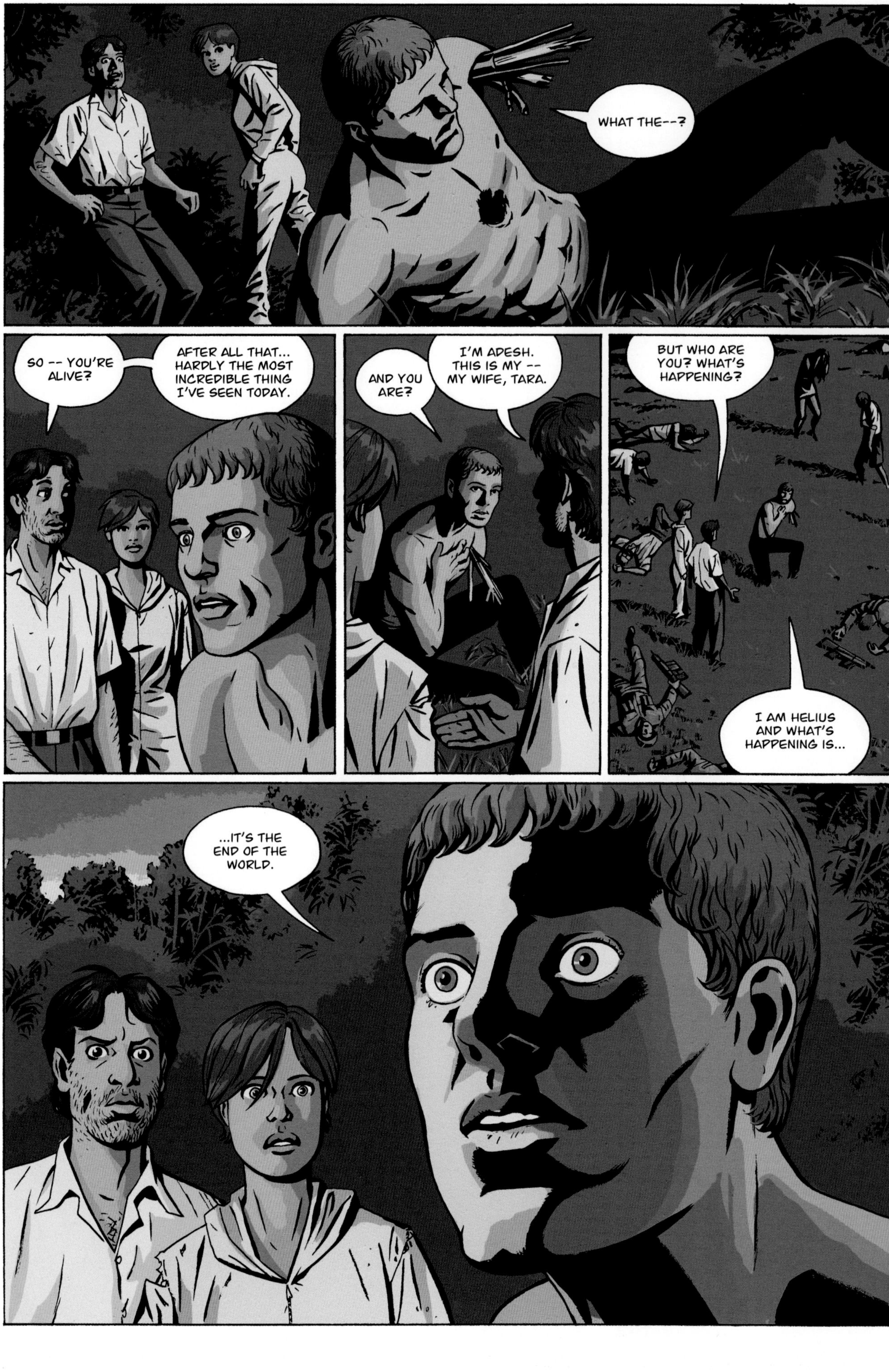
WHAT THE--?
SO -- YOU'RE ALIVE?
AFTER ALL THAT... HARDLY THE MOST INCREDIBLE THING I'VE SEEN TODAY.
AND YOU ARE?
I'M ADESH. THIS IS MY -- MY WIFE, TARA.
BUT WHO ARE YOU? WHAT'S HAPPENING?
I AM HELIUS AND WHAT'S HAPPENING IS...
...IT'S THE END OF THE WORLD.

IN THE NEXT VOLUME OF WORLD WAR X...

WHAT IF THE WORST IS YET TO COME?

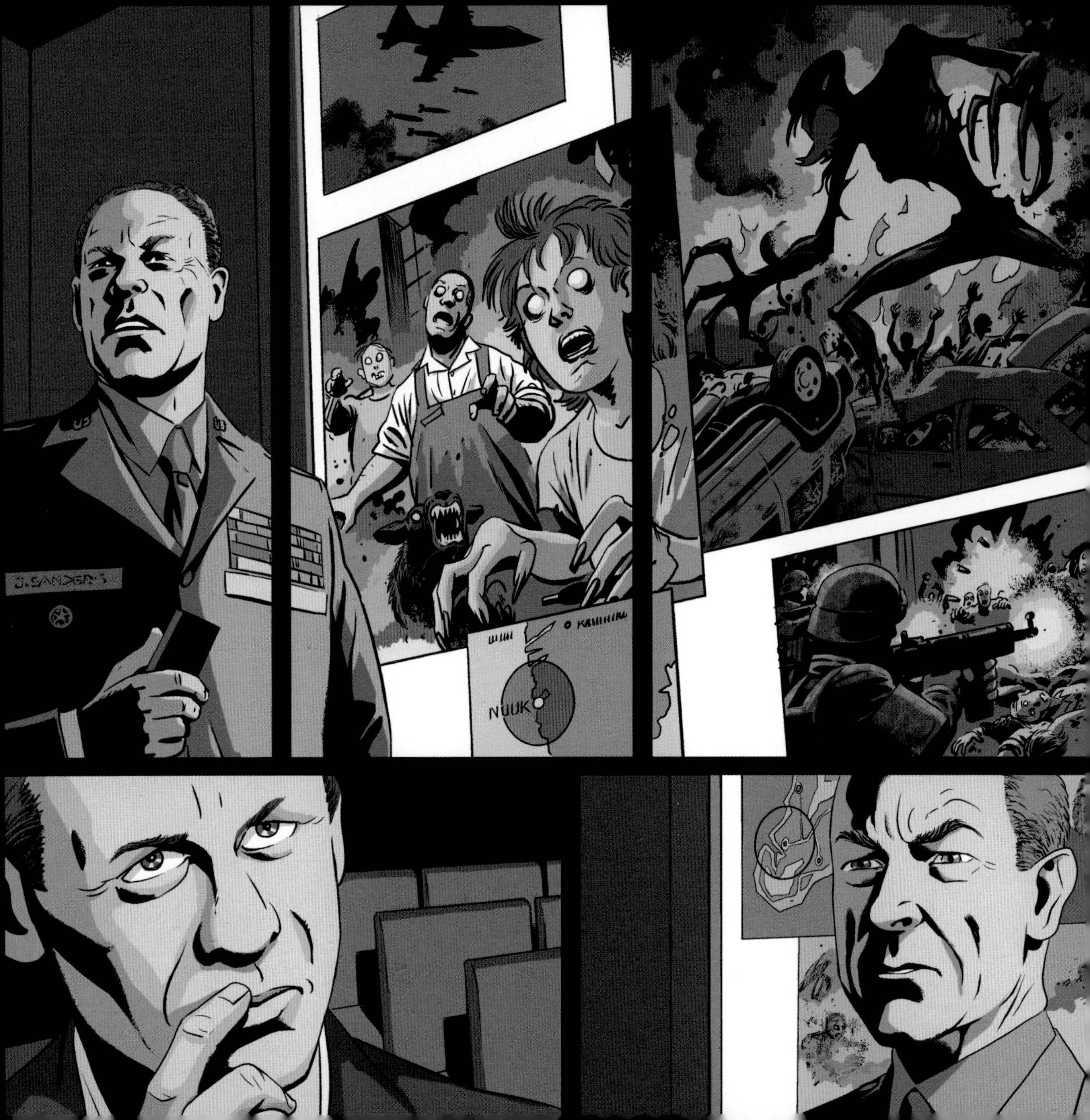
J.SANDERS
NUUK

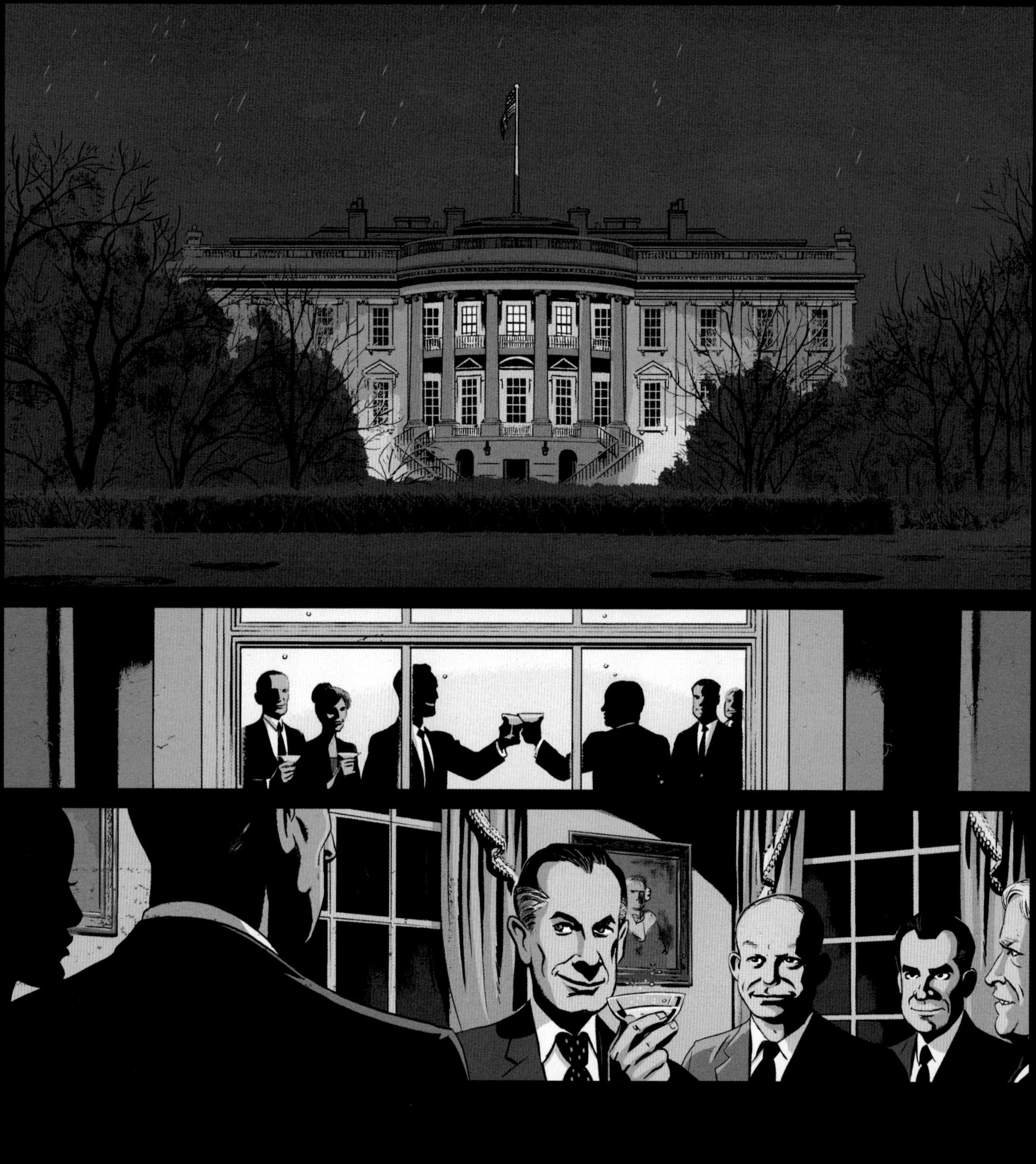

WHAT IF HUMANITY WAS OFFERED AN ENERGY SOURCE SO POWERFUL IT ALLOWED UNPRECEDENTED LEAPS IN TECHNOLOGY...

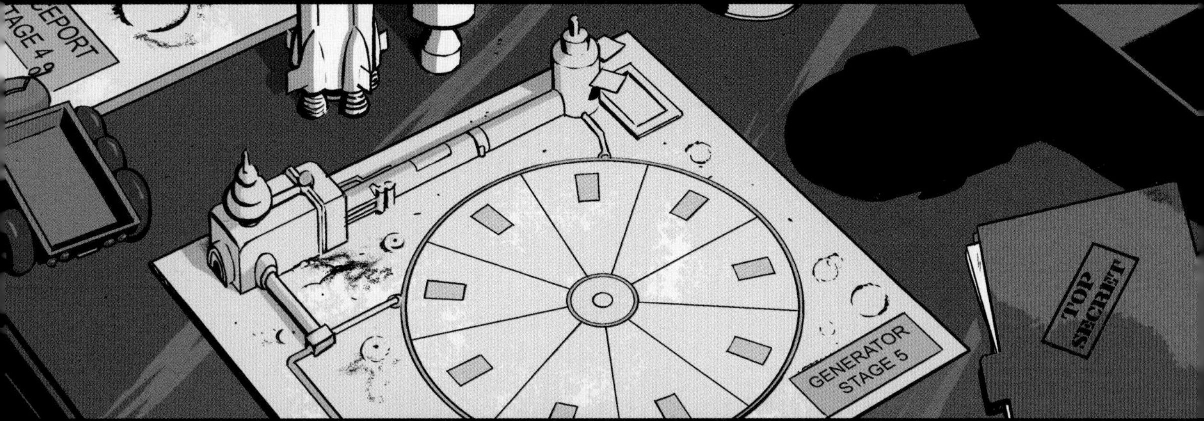
EPORT
TAGE 4
GENERATOR
STAGE 5
TOP
SECRET

BUT THIS ENERGY SOURCE OPENED A STARGATE?

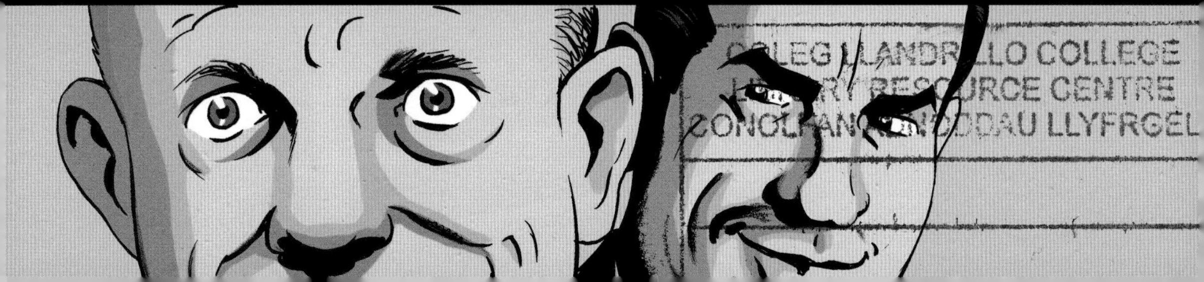

AND WHAT IF IT WAS ALL A TRAP?

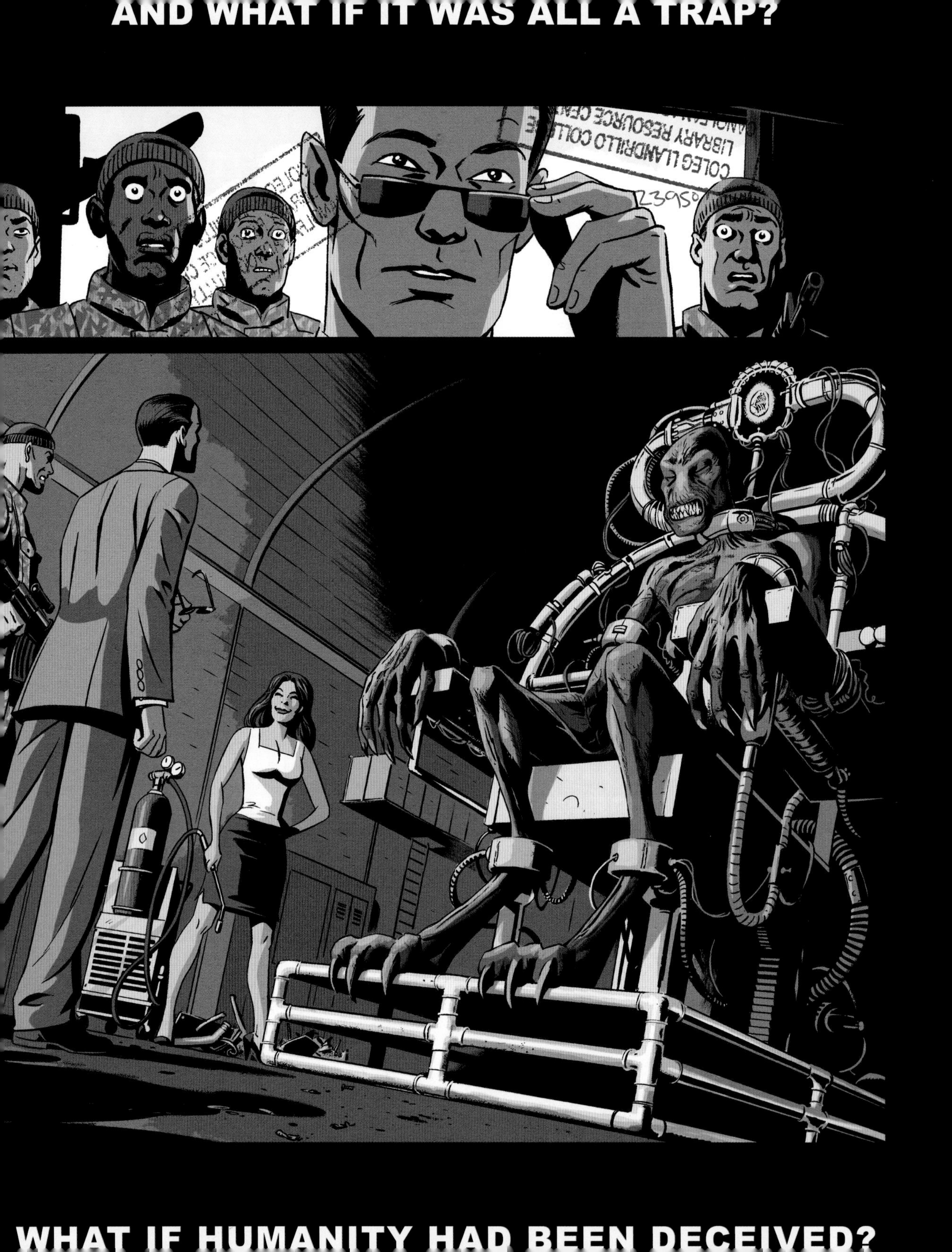

WHAT IF HUMANITY HAD BEEN DECEIVED?

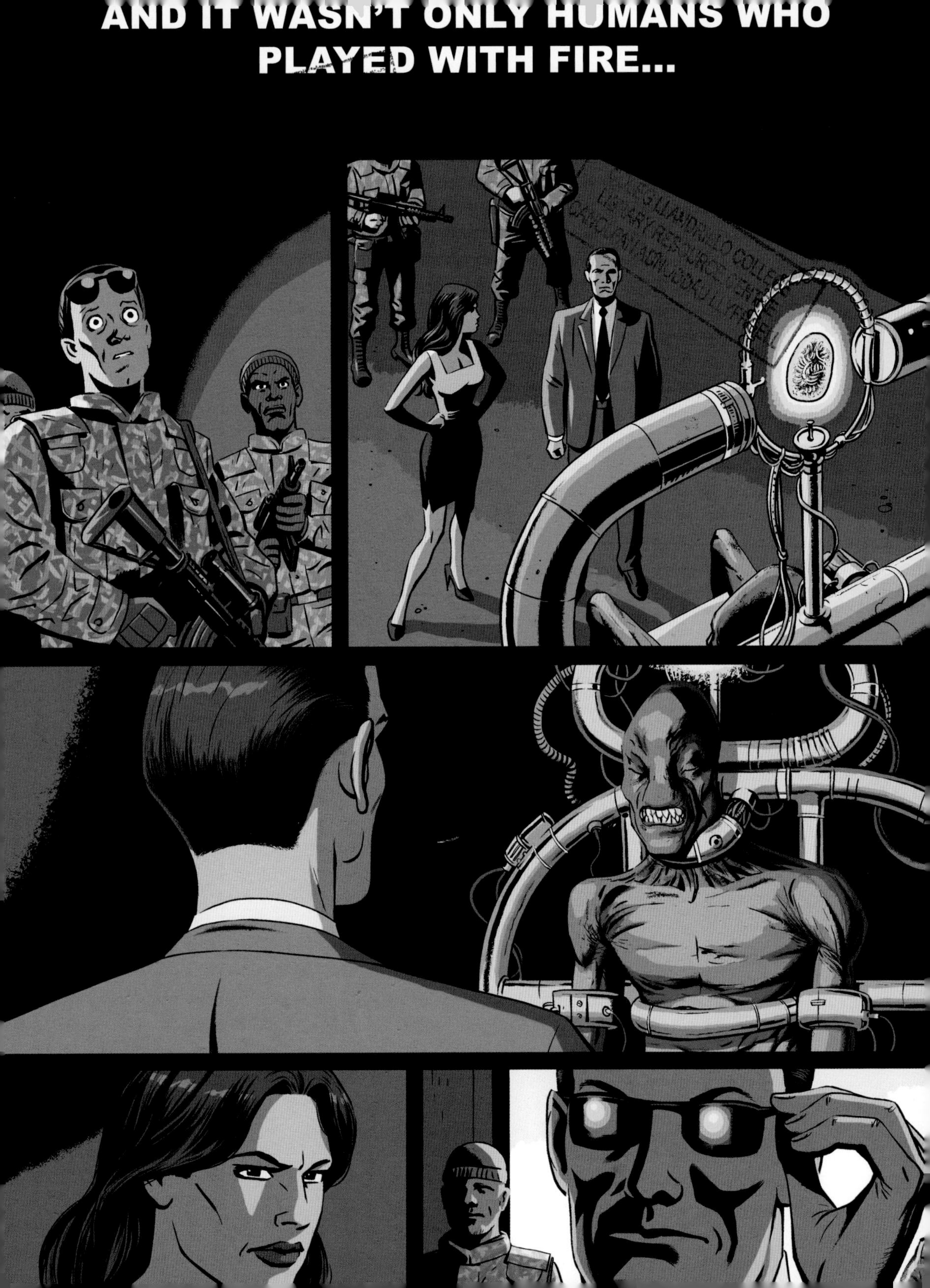
AND IT WASN'T ONLY HUMANS WHO PLAYED WITH FIRE...

**NOW EARTH'S OLDEST INHABITANT
IS ITS ONLY HOPE.**

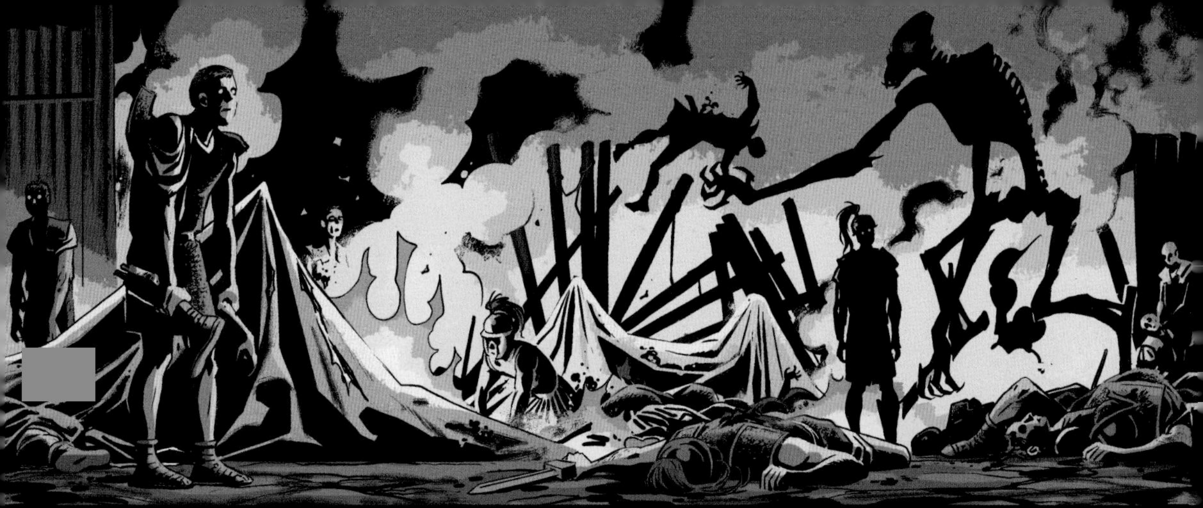

BUT WHO IS HELIUS?
AND WHAT CAN HE DO AGAINST
SUCH A POWERFUL THREAT?

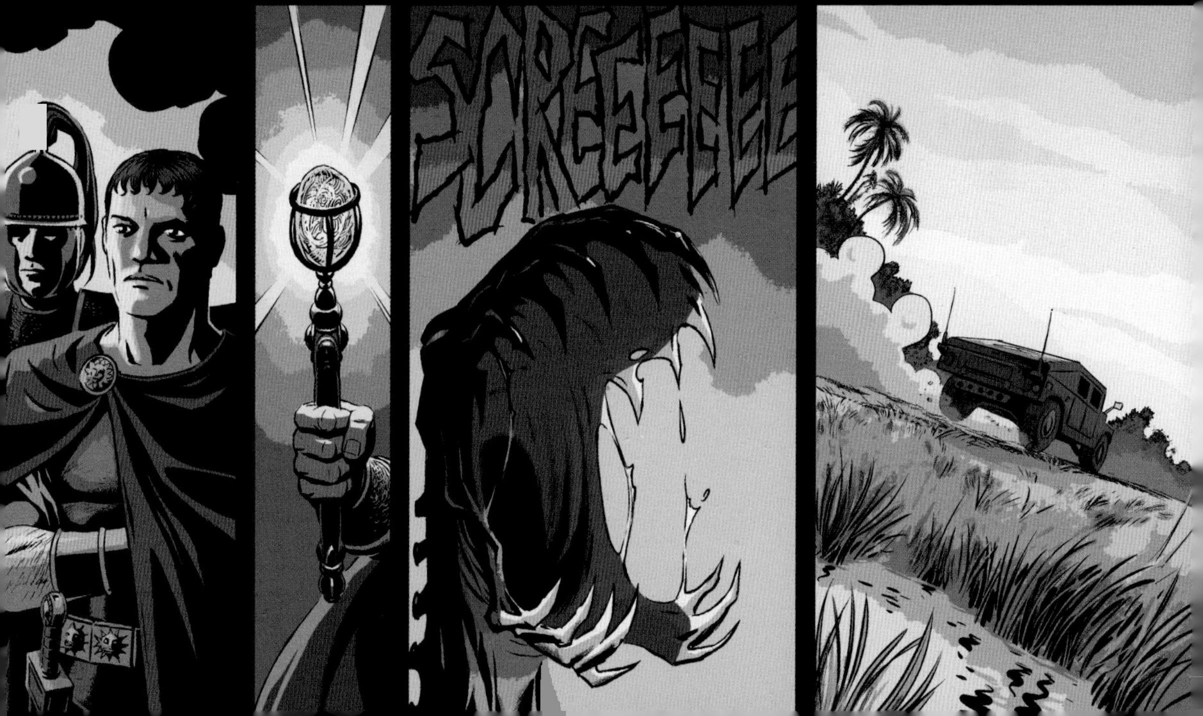
SCREEEEEE

FIND OUT IN THE COMING VOLUMES OF WORLD WAR X!

WORLD
WAR
X
BOOK 2
JERRY FRISSEN / PETER SNEJBJERG

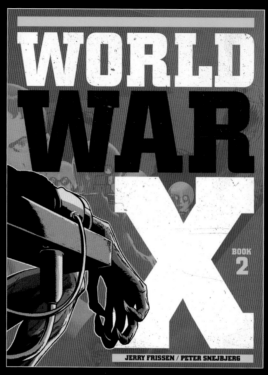

WORLD WAR X: KHARIS
Coming July 2015

WORLD
WAR
X
BOOK 3
JERRY FRISSEN / PETER SNEJBJERG

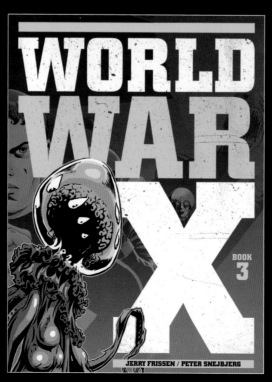

WORLD WAR X: ADESH
Coming October 2015